Who Was Dexter Avenue, Anyhow?

Who Was Dexter Avenue, Anyhow?

Stories Behind the Street Names in Montgomery, Alabama

General Editors
Nancy Grisham Anderson
Blair R. Gaines

Editorial Assistant
Judy Beavers Sims

Researchers and Writers
Ashley Gordon
Nicky Kilmer
Stephanie Larkins
Cindy Mantione
Gwen S. Price
Judy Beavers Sims
Carole K. Whitby

Black Belt Press
Montgomery

The Black Belt Press
P.O. Box 551
Montgomery, AL 36101

Design by Randall Williams

Manufactured in the United States of America

*The Black Belt, defined by its dark, rich soil,
stretches across central Alabama. It was the heart
of the cotton belt. It was and is a place of great
beauty, of extreme wealth and grinding poverty,
of pain and joy. Here we take our stand, listening
to the past, looking to the future.*

For Georgi Rider

Contents

Some Neighborhoods:

Preface

By **NANCY G. ANDERSON** and **BLAIR R. GAINES**
General Editors

Little did Randall Williams, publisher at Black Belt Press, know what an opportunity he was providing when he asked if we knew anyone who might be interested in writing a book on the history of Montgomery street names, a book he was tentatively calling "Who Was Dexter Avenue, Anyhow?"

Since we had individually taught courses in writing, editing, desktop publishing, and book designing, we realized what an invaluable educational opportunity this project could provide for combining the subjects. In the beginning, we planned a two-course sequence. We would devote the first quarter to the research and writing and the second to the editing, design, and layout. We were optimistic and ambitious, if nothing else.

The project proved to be an incredible learning experience for us all, faculty and students alike. We have learned about Montgomery's history and development, planned and unplanned. We have learned new and unique lessons about historical research, particularly where there are few, if any records and documented sources. Thus, we have learned of the importance and liabilities, the values and credibility (or incredibility) of oral history, with all of its charms and flaws.

We have learned about the generosity of people from those who have met with us, to teach us and to learn from us, but most of all to encourage our enthusiasm for this project. We are grateful to many people who have shared their knowledge about our city: Jeff Benton, Tom Connor,

Anita Folmar, Wayne Greenhaw, Jack McLemore, Joe Sadler, and Will Hill Tankersley have all met with the class, some in the classroom and some in places as unlikely as a delicatessen for breakfast or a neighborhood bar for an afternoon of map-reading and reminiscing. Others we met on their own turf: Mary Ann Neeley, at Old Alabama Town; the staff at the Alabama Department of Archives and History, especially Ed Bridges, Debbie Pendleton, Norwood Kerr, and Mark Palmer; and Jerome Ennels and his staff in the Air University Office of History at Maxwell AFB. Some, such as Inge Hill and Camille Elebash-Hill, invited us into their homes for interviews. Many developers, surveyors, and engineers have patiently returned phone calls, sent faxes, and answered countless questions.

These learning experiences have allowed us to savor the joy and rewards of working together on a project that we know, even with its gaps and possible errors, will be a contribution to the city of Montgomery.

We began our research with background reading about the history of Montgomery and surveys of city maps (a comparison of maps printed by various companies reveals how many errors can creep into street names: the 1994 Rand-McNally has Oakland Cemetery instead of Oakwood, to name just one example; and spellings and designations of "street," "avenue," "road" may vary from map to map).

Then came the fundamental task of dividing the thousands of city streets into more or less equal parts, after which—in what became a class joke, and epithet—each student had 363.1111 streets to research. As much as possible, students selected sections of the city in which they had a personal interest.

And then the work really began as students became researchers and writers. They returned again and again to the state archives and to city plat maps to check dates and biographical information. Historical sources for names in the 19th and early 20th centuries were quickly exhausted. Then began the interviewing, the phone calling, the letter-writing.

We soon learned that, at times, like Topsy, Montgomery just grew. Streets in new developments and subdivisions were named by developers and property owners from family names (fathers, mothers, sisters, brothers, children, and perhaps even the beloved family dog); other city phone directories, notably Philadelphia and Tuscaloosa; thematic approaches ("I've always had good luck in a development when I used the word 'wood'" or "I wanted cute, woodsy names"), and numerous other explanations. Often the individuals involved in those naming sessions have only vague memories of the basis of their decisions.

Future researchers will at least be helped by the work of our students who have filled out resource sheets, now deposited in Special Collections at the Auburn University at Montgomery Library, to document the sources they used. The students also developed what one labeled "the one plus one method"—the principle of logical deduction, or combining the time of development with important events or individuals in the city or even the nation or world at the time to deduce the sources for names. In addition, when because of the age of a subdivision or for other reasons the researchers could not pin down the specific intent behind street names, they have used the grouping of similar names in an area as a guide or have noted historical or other connections to a name that may or may not have been intended.

Finally they turned in the identifications on index cards for typing. All the typing, by the way, was done by Georgi Rider, secretary in the AUM Communication Department. She deserves a gold city map, but since we didn't have one, the students dedicated this book to her.

Then came the editing, and as a group, we made the following arbitrary decisions to guide our work:

- the official list of streets from the City of Montgomery, updated through May 1995, has been used for all spellings and labels ("street," "avenue," "lane," etc.);
- the streets included are restricted to those inside the city limits (rather than the police jurisdiction), with a few exceptions for streets with fascinating stories;
- all private streets are excluded, except for a few with intriguing stories;
- the alphabetizing is literal letter by letter without regard to whether the entry is one word or more, and the label of "road," "street," etc., has been ignored in the overall alphabetizing (*e.g.*, "Vaughn Rd." appears before "Vaughn Park Rd.").
- streets with directional labels ("N.," "S.," "E.," "W.") are alphabetized under the primary word in the street name with directions following to show the details; the only exceptions are where the direction seems to be part of the name itself, such as "South Hampton";
- if there are multiple explanations for the origin of a name, we have recorded all *credible* versions—as funny and charming as were some of the tall tales, we regretfully excluded them;
- named streets for which we could find no information are denoted by a †. Some others for which we had no specific information are identified by groupings of similar names (for example, "In a neighborhood using women's first names").

We hope readers will come forward with more information, even better stories, and additions and corrections for future editions of this book. To that end, please see page 214 for directions on writing to us.

Acknowledgments

Hundreds of individuals provided information, suggestions, or leads for this book. A few who worked closely with us have already been named in the preface. In addition, the following persons were especially generous of their time in meeting with us, sharing stories, or giving us information from their own files and research.

Owen Aronov
Bowen and Carol Ballard
June Belle
Rickey Best
Dot Cramton
Gene Davis
Donald B. Dodd
Robert Forbus
Herman and Anne Franco
Robert Heilpern
Catherine Jones
Carol King
Bob Lamar
Jimmy Lowder
Lisa Martin
Nancy Maynard
Billy McLemore
Jack McLemore
Patricia Morgan
Charles Nicrosi
William Nicrosi, Jr.

Tommy Nolen
Felix Norman
John Parker
Edward Pattillo
Pep Pilgreen
Haygood Poundstone
Harold Price
Joe Reed
Craig Sheldon
Dan Stallings
Daryl Strickland
Margaret Swearingen
Billy Turner
Ken Upchurch
Art Wallace
Joe Watkins
Ted Watts
Jerry Wills
Fred Woolard
George Wright

Named Streets

■ Indicates neighborhood or subdivision
† Indicates no information available

A

Aaron Street
Developer and Realtor Aaron Aronov.

Abbie Street
One of several downtown streets named for women and located in an industrial area near the Alabama River.

Aberdeen Drive (E. & W.)
A city in Scotland; in a neighborhood using British names.

Acacia Court
Tropical tree with white or yellow flowers.

Ada Court
In a neighborhood of streets using women's first names.

Adams Place, Street
Pl.: On Maxwell AFB. St.: John Adams (1735-1826), second president of the U.S. The 6th U.S. president, John Quincy Adams, deeded much of what is now Montgomery to the Vickers family in 1827. See Van Allen Dr.

Adele Street
In a neighborhood of several streets named for people.

Adeline Street
In a neighborhood of streets named for people.

Adler Road †

Adler Street
On Maxwell AFB, probably named in honor of Capt. Elmer E. Adler, who graduated with Class I, 1931-32, of the Air Corps Tactical School. The school was moved from Langley Field, Va., in 1931 and was considered critical to the country's defense. It breathed new life into Maxwell Field and helped to transform the facility from a deteriorating WWI depot into a modern military base.

Adrian Lane
In a series of parallel streets with references to Avalon, Wedgewood, Druid Hills. Of interest: a short form of the name of Emperor Hadrian (117-38 A.D.).

Agate Street
A fine-grained mineral with colored bands and clouding.

Agnew Street
Prev. Woodrow St. Walter D. Agnew, Huntingdon College President from 1922-1938, noted for his leadership during the Depression.

Aimee Drive
Aimee Thomason, wife of contractor M.R. Thomason.

Ainsworth Court, Drive †
A Nebraska county and name of a 1947 Nobel Prize winner.

Air Base Boulelvard
Prev. Western Blvd. Leads to Maxwell AFB.

Airwood Drive
A reference to the breeze that flows through the woods and is so refreshing in the hot Montgomery summertime.

Ajax Street
Parallel to Hercules St. Named as part of the Hugh Simpson subdivision in 1907. Ajax, hero of the Trojan War, helped Odysseus rescue the corpse of Achilles.

Alabama Street
Alibamu (thicket clearers), a small local Indian tribe from which the state took its name. Gen. John Scott, one of Montgomery's founders, also named his settlement, East Alabama Town, for the tribe.

Alabama Christian Drive (W.)
Once adjacent to Alabama Christian College, which was renamed as Faulkner University on July 18, 1985.

Aladena Drive
Fanciful joining of "Ala" and "dena," possibly part of a person's name.

Alamo Drive
The famous mission in San Antonio where, in March 1836, Davey Crockett, Jim Bowie, William Travis and others fought the heroic battle against the Mexican General Santa Anna and his troops during the Texas Revolution.

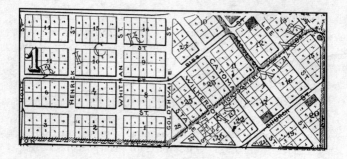

Why Downtown Streets Don't Meet: The Street Conflict

Montgomery's downtown streets, which collide at an angle near the river, are a mysterious maze to new residents and visitors. For this irritating enigma, there are two men at whom we can point our fingers: Andrew Dexter and John Scott.

After the 1814 Battle of Horseshoe Bend made this area relatively safe from hostile Indians, the United States government had the 20 million acres received from the Creeks surveyed and sold at auction. At the Milledgeville, Ga., sale in 1817, Andrew Dexter made the minimum 5 percent down payment on the southern half of a section of land, and John Scott, representing a group of investors, bought a quarter of a section nearby.

Dexter and John Falconer (see "The Forgotten Founder") established a town and named it New Philadelphia, laying out the streets to run east to west. Scott also established a town on his portion and named it Alabama, laying out his streets to run northeast to southwest.

The two towns were rivals from the start. Scott's town was subject to flooding and plagued with mosquitoes and Dexter's town was more attractive to new settlers. Scott purchased more land even closer to New Philadelphia and named it East Alabama. By then, the two men had become bitter combatants, and the streets in Scott's new town were arranged as before to keep them from joining Dexter's streets.

New arrivals via the Old Federal Road came first to New Philadelphia, were informed of the disadvantages of East Alabama and persuaded to settle in Dexter's town. Scott countered by blocking all access to the river. New Philadelphia attracted the merchants and was soon a booming town, while East Alabama was mostly residential. When the dying town of Fort Jackson decided to give up the county seat, the rivalry intensified as both towns competed for the honor. East Alabama won that battle and became the center of county government.

Finally on Dec. 3, 1819, the two towns agreed to a merger and built a new courthouse where they joined. They also agreed on a new name [see Montgomery St.]. The newly united town of Montgomery had only 401 residents, 40 percent of whom were slaves. Although Dexter and Scott had resolved their differences, the odd joining of streets could not be corrected since by that time houses and business establishments had been erected along their lengths.

Alamont Drive

A combination of "Alabama" and "Montgomery."

Alan Lane

Son of Don Martin, a local real estate developer.

Alatex Road

Alatex Corp., a shirt manufacturing company.

Albans Lane

St. Albans was a crucial battle during the English Wars of the Roses that gave control to the Yorkists (1455).

Albemarle Road

County in Va. This road parallels Chevy Chase Dr., a suburb of Washington, D.C., near Va.

Alderpoint Drive

See Heatherton Heights.

Alduc Court

Mr. Alduc, a local engineer, suggested a street be named for him.

Alexander Street

William Anthony Alexander (1837-1914), an English immigrant who invented and created the *Hunley*, the 1st submarine used in the Civil War in 1864. The *Hunley* attacked the Union ship *Housatonic* in Charleston Harbor and both sank.

Alfred Street

In a neighborhood of streets using men's and women's first names.

Alison Drive

In a neighborhood of streets with first names, many of them women's.

Allendale Place, Road

Allen family, local landowners. See Woodley Rd.

Allen's Trail

Allen McLemore, the youngest son of Jack McLemore, a local landowner and businessman.

Alma Drive

Possibly for the community in Clarke Co. that is named for Alma Flinn from Barlow Bend, who was that community's first school teacher.

Alpine Drive

While Montgomery's topography boasts no mountains, this

pleasant street name brings to mind height and cool breezes that are particularly welcome here during the hot, humid summertime.

Alred Court
For Carl Alred, the vice president and financial officer of Aronov Realty.

Alsop Street
Thomas J. Alsop, who was a wealthy Montgomery brick yard owner of the post Civil War era.

Alta Road
Possibly referring to terms for Calif., a state once thought to be an island: "Baja" is lower California and "Alta" is the rest of the mainland. "Alta" generally refers to height or altitude.

Althea Street
One of a series of streets in the Lee High School area named by 1920s developers for women, natural features and family names.

Amanda Loop, Lane
Prev. Amanda Lenore Dr. (now the name of a street outside city limits). Possibly one of George R. Clayton's children.

Amberly Road
See Regency Park.

Amelia Street
See Highland Gardens.

Amherst Drive
Amherst College was founded in 1825 at Amherst, Mass., and had its beginning in lessons there by Congregationalist clergyman-professor Zephaniah Swift Moore.

Amity Lane
In a region of English-sounding names, this is an English term for friendship.

Amos Street
Amos Miller, the son of Ed and Clara Miller, who were close friends of Fred Cramton, the developer of Highland Gardens. See Cramton Bowl and Highland Gardens.

Amoy Court
See Highland Gardens.

Andalusia Street
Prev. Third St. A small town in S. Ala.

Anderson Court, Street

John Crawford Anderson, attorney, circuit judge in the first judicial circuit from 1895-1904 and chief justice of the Alabama Supreme Court from 1914-1916.

Andova Drive

Also spelled "Andover" on some maps. A town in N.E. Mass., home of Andover Academy.

Andre Street †

Andrews Street

Prev. 10th St. on Maxwell AFB, renamed to honor Lt. Gen. Frank M. Andrews. He was a 1928 graduate of the Air Corps Tactical School; Commanding Officer of General HQ AF, 1935; Air Officer of the 8th Corps Area, 1939; CO of the Panama Canal AF, 1940; CO of Caribbean Defense Command, 1941; CO of U.S. Air Forces in the Middle East, 1942; and Commanding General of U.S. Forces in the European Theatre, 1943. He was killed in an airplane accident on May 3, 1943.

Ann Street

Prev. Evergreen St. The name was probably changed in the late 1930s by the Houghtons, who owned a farm and mansion at the corner of what is now the Atlanta Hwy. and Ann St., in honor of their daughter Ann. At the time, neighborhood children called it "Plum Nelly" because it was "plum out of town and nearly out in the country."

Anna Place†

Anne Arbor Place

Probably for Ann Arbor, Mich., although spelled differently.

Anthony Street

Possibly for Micajah Anthony, one of the original land purchasers at the Milledgeville, Ga., sale of Montgomery area land.

Antoinette Drive

Possibly for Marie Antoinette, who was beheaded in Paris on Oct. 16, 1793, along with her husband, Louis XVI, during the French Revolution. Ironically, it was backing the American Revolution that helped to bankrupt France and foment revolution there.

Anton Drive (N. & S.)

Anton Haardt, the daughter of a local real estate developer, John H. Haardt.

Apache Court

An American Indian tribe, related to the Navajo, who settled in southwestern New Mexico and western Texas after migrating from Canada. See Arrowhead.

Applecross Place

See Young Place.

Apple Jack Court

Developed in the area of a former orchard, where streets are named for that theme.

Apple Orchard Street

See Apple Jack Court.

Applewood Court

In a neighborhood of streets with tree names.

April Court, Street †

Arba Street

The initials of the Alabama Road Builders Association.

Arborfield Road

See "Montgomery's Own Philadelphia Story."

Arbor Glen Drive

Near an area of apple-themed streets around the Alabama Shakespeare Festival and across the bypass from the Young farm area.

Arbor Station Road

Although named before the Young Farm Development, it is near an apple-themed section in that area.

Arden Road

Fanciful forest in which fairies cavort in Shakespeare's *Midsummer Night's Dream*.

Ardmore Drive

A city in Pa. located outside of Philadelphia. This drive is among a series of streets named in alphabetical order from Ardmore to Esmond.

Argyle Road

A county in western Scotland, from which the Clan Campbell's distinctive tartan took its name.

Arlington Road

Robert E. Lee's home in N. Va., for which the surrounding county was named. This county was part of the District of Columbia from 1790 to 1847.

Arnold Street

Prev. 1st St., on Maxwell AFB, renamed to honor Gen. Henry H. "Hap" Arnold. He served as assistant Chief of the Air Corps in 1936; Chief of the Air Corps in 1938; and Chief of the Army Air Force in 1941. He was appointed Commanding General of the Allied Air Forces in 1942. He was promoted to General of the Air Force and remains the USAF's only five-star general. He died on Jan. 15, 1950.

Aronov Avenue

Aaron Aronov and his real estate company.

■ ARROWHEAD

Originally a golf course, the subdivision was added later. Streets were given Indian names after broken pottery and arrowheads found near a creek on the eastern boundary.

Arrowhead Court, Drive

See Arrowhead.

Arrowhead Forest Court, Drive

See Arrowhead West.

■ ARROWHEAD WEST

Once farm and pasture land; the street names denote country themes.

Arrowleaf Court, Place, Road

See Arrowhead West.

Arthur Street

An active supporter for the development of Capitol Heights. In a neighborhood of streets named for people. Of interest: Chester A. Arthur, the 21st U.S. president, held an auction while he was in office and disposed of all the historic furniture. He died of a stroke in 1886.

Asbury Lane

See "Montgomery's Own Philadelphia Story." Located in a neighborhood of English-themed names. Of note: Francis Asbury, born in England, was the first Methodist-Episcopal bishop in the American colonies.

Ash Street
See Maxwell AFB.

Ashburton Drive
Of note: The Webster-Ashburton Treaty of 1842 settled some long-standing border disputes between the U.S. and Canada. The two neighboring nations have since settled their disputes peacefully.

Ashlawn Drive
The Charlottesville, Va., home of the 5th U.S. president, James Monroe (1758-1831), who issued the Monroe Doctrine in 1923, an important principle of foreign policy.

Ashley Avenue, Road
Ave.: For F.L. Ashley, a local planter. Rd.: For area developers John and Albert Ashley.

Ashridge Drive
Generic.

Ashton Circle, Court, Road †

Ashwood Circle, Court
Descriptive, generic.

Aspen Lane
Near White Acres Rd., named for a white-barked tree whose leaves flutter in the wind and appear silver because of their unusual attachment to the branches.

Astrid Place (W.)
Retired Col. Hugh Hughes, a West Point graduate employed by Ballard Realty, gave several streets in Woodmere feminine German names. See Greta Pl., Heidi Pl. and Helga Pl.

Atasi Drive
Atasi or Autosee; ancient upper Creek town in Macon County; derived from Creek "a'tass" (war club).

Atlanta Highway
Until construction of the Eisenhower Interstate System's route 85 through Montgomery, this highway was the primary route to Atlanta.

Atom Street
In an area annexed in 1910. Probably named for the particle. One of a series of downtown streets located in an industrial area near the Alabama River and a railroad.

Auburn Street

Auburn, Ala., home of Auburn University. It is parallel to Troy St., home of Troy State University.

Audubon Road

John James Audubon (1785-1851), American naturalist, painter, and author of *The Birds of America*, a classic of science and art.

Augusta Avenue, Place

Augusta Sedberry Thomas, the grandmother of property owner Jett Thomas.

Austin Street

See Highland Gardens.

Autume Lane

Middle English and Latin spellings of "autumn" have this root.

Avalon Lane

In Arthurian legend, Avalon is an island paradise in the western seas to which King Arthur went at his death.

Avenue A

A short portion of the original street, most of which has been redesignated as Morris Avenue. Located on Gunter Annex of Maxwell AFB. See Maxwell AFB.

Avenue F

See Maxwell AFB.

Avenue L

A one-block street west of I-65.

Avon Court, Road

A river in England that flows to the Severn and is best known for its association with Shakespeare.

Avondale Court, Road

One of a series of streets in the Perry Hills subdivision ending with "dale."

Aylsbury Place

Located near Wiltshire and Bristol among other English-sounding names.

Azalea Drive

A flowering shrub in various colors prevalent in many Montgomery neighborhoods such as Cloverdale, Dalraida and the Garden District.

B

Babette Circle
In an area with women's first names used for several streets.

Babsdale Chase
See Wynlakes.

Baffin Court, Drive
See Highland Gardens.

Bainbridge Street (N. & S.)
William Bainbridge, a naval commodore of the War of 1812 who is noted for his defeat of the British ship *Java.*

Baker Avenue, Street
Ave: Prev. Avenue B, on Gunter Annex of Maxwell AFB, renamed to honor F/C W.B. Baker, the second American to die while stationed at Gunter Field. He was killed on Jan. 31, 1941. St.: Located in a neighborhood of streets named for people.

Balboa Road
The Spanish explorer Vasco de Balboa (1475-1517).

Baldwin Avenue
Possibly for Dr. B. J. Baldwin, grandson of early settler Frank Barnett. See Barnett Rd. Also a county in S. Ala. named for Sen. Abraham Baldwin of Ga.

Baldwin Brook Court, Drive
In an area between Hannon Slough and Baldwin Slough, where several streets have "brook" in their names.

Balfour Road
Of interest: Arthur James Balfour was the British statesman who crafted the Balfour Declaration establishing support for a Jewish homeland in Palestine. Also, possibly for Balfour of Burley, a character in Walter Scott's novel, *Old Morality.* London *Times* correspondent William Russel mentions this character in an article written in Montgomery on May 6, 1861.

Ballentine Drive
Developed by Paul Corwin and named for a type of beer.

Balmoral Road
For Balmoral Castle, the summer home of the British royal family; also, an attractive street in the Mountain Brook subdivision of Birmingham.

Banbury Avenue
A city in England located due south of Birmingham.

Bancroft Avenue
Perhaps for George Bancroft (1800-1891), American historian and Secretary of the Navy (1845-46), who established the U.S. Naval Academy.

Bangor Court
Cities in Maine and Northern Ireland.

Bank Street
In a neighborhood of streets named for people.

Bankhead Avenue
Marie Bankhead Owen and the Bankhead family, which includes senators, historians and actress Tallulah Bankhead.

Banyan Drive
A tropical Indian fig tree planted for ornament and shade. Its roots often grow visibly above ground.

Barby Road †

Barksdale Street
See Highland Gardens. On Maxwell AFB, probably honoring Lt. Eugene H. Barksdale, who was killed in an aircraft accident in the 1920s.

Barley Drive
Dan Barley, the office manager for area developer A.F. Woolard.

Barnes Street
Prev. 11th St. on Maxwell AFB, it was renamed to honor Lt. Gen. Earl W. Barnes. He was a graduate of the Air Corps Tactical School, 1937; ACTS Instructor, 1937-40; Commanding General of the 13th Fighter Command, 1943; and CO of the 13th AF, 1945. He enjoyed prestigious assignments with the Far East Command and the UN Command after WWII. A second street is located just east of the base and was named by Joe Sadler for O.E. Barnes, the former superintendent of mails in Montgomery.

Barnett Road
Possibly for early settlers Frank and Charles Barnett. Frank Barnett was the father of Hon. Joel Barnett and the grandfather of Dr. B. J. Baldwin.

Bassett Court, Drive †

Bay Street
See Oak Park and Maxwell AFB.

Bayberry Street
An aromatic tree or shrub. See Pecan Grove Estates.

Beach Street
Possibly for the cooling idea of a south Alabama beach, but more likely for a local family since it is in a neighborhood of streets named for people.

Beacon Drive
Descriptive, generic.

Beardsley Drive †

Beaumont Drive
French word for "beautiful mountain/hill."

Beauregard Street
Possibly for Confederate Gen. Pierre Gustave Toutant Beauregard (1818-1893). Also, a community in Lee County.

Beauvoir Lake Court, Drive
Name of Jefferson Davis' plantation in Mississippi. Employees of the development company participated in a contest to name this street. Beauvoir was also the former name of the Montgomery Country Club, established in 1865.

Beck Court
Lee Hill Beck, daughter of W. Inge Hill, Sr., and her husband, James Beck. Situated in an area formerly owned by W.H. Vaughan, Corrie Hill Tankersley and the W. Inge Hill, Sr., family.

Beckview Drive
In a neighborhood with several streets named for people.

Beckwith Road
Situated in a neighborhood with streets named for people.

Bedford Lane
See "Montgomery's Own Philadelphia Story."

Beech Street
See Maxwell AFB. Ironically, although named for the tree, this is also the name of the manufacturer of the T-34A aircraft used in USAF training units during the 1950s.

Beechdale Road
One of a series of streets near Perry Hills subdivision ending with "dale."

Beecher Street

Named by J.H. Shreve in 1906, possibly for the family of L.T. Beecher, secretary-treasurer of the Tennessee Coal, Iron & Railroad Co., of Birmingham, Ala.

Beeline Street

Located off U.S. Hwy 31 N. A straight route to Birmingham, the highway is often referred to as the Beeline Hwy. When the area was developed, the street was given the highway's nickname. The Beeline Hwy. was the first long road in the state to be paved. It extended from Ardmore (near Athens) to Mobile.

Belcher Drive

S.E. Belcher, the chairman of the board of Southern United Life Insurance Co.

Belfast Street

A seaport, capital of Northern Ireland.

Bell Chase, Circle, Gables

While Bell Rd. is the best-known of these, there are several streets in S.E. Montgomery that are named for the N.J. Bell estate.

Bell Road, Street

Rd.: See Bell Chase. St.: Prev. Cahaba St. Alexander and William B. Bell, Montgomery pioneers and merchants on Market St., now Dexter Ave. N.J. Bell, Sr., Lowndes County plantation owner, moved to Montgomery in 1891. Shortly after the turn of the century, he built Alabama's tallest building (12 floors). The street was the first location of Auburn University at Montgomery.

Bell Creek Court

See Bell Chase.

Belleau Drive

A forested area of northern France where Allies won a key WWI victory; now the site of an American cemetery.

Bellehurst Drive

See "Montgomery's Own Philadelphia Story."

Bellgate Court

Proximity to Bell Rd.

Bell Grove Place

See Bell Chase.

Bellinger Lane

The owner of this land in 1860, that is now a part of Burtonville subdivision,was Carnot Bellinger (1806-1876), a Montgomery physician, and his wife, Sarah Bozier Hails Bellinger. The first president of the Montgomery Hospital Association, he established and donated the "First Soldier's Home," a hospital for Confederate soldiers during the war. He is buried in Oakwood Cemetery.

Bellmont Court

See Bell Chase.

Bell Road Court

See Bell Chase.

■ BELL STATION

Developed by John Foshee and John Bowman, this subdivision is adjacent to Bell Rd. and has a railroad theme.

Bellwood Drive

A combination of Bell Rd. and a pastoral theme.

Belmont Street

Possibly for the Belmont family, which included Alva Erskine Smith Belmont, an Ala. socialite and suffragette.

Belvedere Drive

The name of the palace that became the Vatican Museum; also, a gazebo.

Belview Street

Named as part of the Issac Winters plat in 1887. Possible combination of the name Bell or Bellinger, local property owners, and "view."

Belvoir Road

From two French words, meaning "pretty to see." Ft. Belvoir, Va., also bears this name.

Benbow Court †

Ben's Alley

A Carol Villa street named for area landowner Wiley Pearson Johnson's son, Ben.

Bennett Drive

See Forest Hills.

Bennington Court

The developer "liked the name."

Bent Brook Drive
See Wynlakes.

Bent Tree Drive
In section of streets bearing tree names in Halcyon South.

Bentley Court
A British automobile. The street is located in Copperfield, an area of British-inspired names.

Berkley Drive
For the once-popular song, "A Nightingale Sang in Berkeley Square," although it is spelled differently.

Berkshire Court, Drive
A popular vacation area in western Mass., named for wooded hills.

Berwick Drive
Scottish town that was the site of sieges and battles in the Middle Ages; in a series of streets with names in alphabetical order from Ardmore to Esmond.

Beth Manor Drive †

Beverly Drive
Among several streets named for people.

Bibb Street
William Wyatt Bibb was the only governor of the Alabama Territory (1817-1819), and the first governor of the State of Alabama (1819-1820). His brother, Thomas Bibb, was Ala.'s second governor (1820-21); and their brother, John Dandridge Bibb, was a member of the Alabama Constitutional Convention of 1819.

Bibb Graves Avenue
A Montgomery native and governor of Ala.(1927-31, 1935-39).

Bienville Road
Jean-Baptiste Le Moyne de Bienville, the French governor of Mobile in the early 1700s. He is noted for paying Swiss mercenaries to live at Ft. Toulouse in 1733.

Bigfield Road
See Arrowhead West.

Billings Street
A town in Montana located on the banks of the Yellowstone River.

Biltmore Avenue

A Vanderbilt family summer estate near Asheville, N.C., that was completed in 1895. It is the world's largest private home.

Birch Street

A deciduous forest tree found in temperate areas of the northern hemisphere.

Birdwood Court, Drive

Descriptive, generic.

Birmingham Highway

A portion of U.S. Hwy. 31 that connects Montgomery to Birmingham. See Beeline St.

Biscayne Drive

A narrow inlet of the Atlantic Ocean in southwest Florida, near Miami.

Bishop Street

In a neighborhood of streets named for people. Possibly for Borum Bishop, co-founder of Bishop-Parker Furniture Co. in the 1930s.

Bitford Way †

Blackburn Avenue

An English textile-manufacturing city.

Blackshear Drive †

Blackwood Drive

Located in a wooded area.

Blair Place

For Algernon Blair, local contractor.

Blairwood

See Blair Place.

Blake Street †

Bluegrass Stakes

In a neighborhood of streets with names derived from horse racing. See Taylor Crossing.

Blushing Groom

In a neighborhood of streets with names derived from horse racing. See Taylor Crossing.

Blythewood Road

Among a group of streets with "wood" as part of their names: Charing Wood, Saddlewood, Hollowwood; near Forest Ridge.

Boat Road

An old access road from Old Selma Rd. that leads to a launch area on Catoma Creek.

Bobby Lane

In a neighborhood of streets with men's and women's first names.

Bolingbrook Lane

Henry Bolingbroke (Bolinbrook), who became Henry IV of England; a character in Shakespeare's history plays. See "Wynton M. Blount Cultural Park."

Bolivar Street

A South American revolutionary leader who defeated the Spanish in 1819. Venezuelan currency is named for him.

Bolton Drive

A borough of northwest England located northwest of Manchester. It was a center of the woolen trade from the 14th to the 18th century. It is in an area where several streets are named for people, such as Endover and Fleming.

Bonfield Court, Drive

See Regency Park.

Bonnie Crest Court

A short road bisecting the Bonnie Crest Country Club grounds. A family enclave is located on this short street.

Booker Street

Honors Booker T. Washington (1856-1915), reformer, educator, author and lecturer. Located near Carver St.

Boone Street

In a neighborhood of streets named for people, this one may honor frontiersman Daniel Boone, who, in reply to a question, said: "No, I can't say as ever I was lost, but I was bewildered once for three days."

Boswell Road

Of interest: James Boswell is famous for his lengthy biography of Samuel Johnson. Johnson once remarked to Boswell: "You have but two topics, yourself and me, and I'm sick of both." Among several streets that are named for people.

Boultier Street

Prev. Frederick St. Possibly renamed to honor L. K. Boultier, a benefactor of the Working Woman's Home Association.

Bournesmouth Drive

In a neighborhood of streets with English references, probably a variant of Bournemouth, a resort area in southern England situated on an inlet of the English Channel southwest of Southampton.

Bowen Drive

Thomas Bowen Hill, a Montgomery attorney.

Bowling Green Drive

A university near Toledo, Ohio, founded in 1910. See College Grove.

Bowman Street

Prev. Stuart St., it was probably renamed in memory of Edward Bowman, a popular drum major for the Lanier High School band, who was killed during WWII.

Boxwood Drive

A popular ornamental shrub that was used in landscaping this street.

Boyce Street

An active supporter for the development of Capitol Heights.

Boyd Street

See Highland Gardens.

■ BOYLSTON

The streets in this industrial neighborhood were named by officials of the West Boylston Manufacturing Co., which relocated to the Montgomery area in the 1930s from Boylston, Mass. The area was once part of "Forest Farms," owned by Col. Albert J. Pickett. Around the turn of the century, it became known as "Pickett Springs" and was the favorite swimming hole and picnic spot for city dwellers. Pickett Springs closed prior to WWI, when that area became the location of Camp Sheridan, a large U.S. Army training facility.

Boys Club Road

The location of the Highland Village Youth Center.

Bozeman Drive †

Brackenbury Place

Robert Brakenbury, the historical figure and character in Shakespeare's *Richard III*. See "Wynton M. Blount Cultural Park."

Braddock Road

In the 1930s and '40s, this land was the White cattle farm; Mr. White owned White Roofing Co., an enterprise that is still in business today.

Bradford Place

Located near Technapark.

Bradley Drive

One of a series of streets in the Lee High School area named by 1920s developers for women's names, natural features and family names.

Braeburn Road

In a neighborhood of Scottish-themed street names. "Brae" means "a steep bank next to a river valley."

Bragg Street

Prev. Caffy St. and later Patrick St., it was renamed for Walter Lawrence Bragg (1835-1891), a Harvard law graduate and Montgomery lawyer elected chairman of the Democratic Election Committee in 1871. He was instrumental in ending the rule of the carpetbaggers in Alabama.

Brampton Court (S.), Lane

In Copperfield, an area of British-themed names. The English home of John Elliott, founder of Brampton, Ontario.

Brantford Boulevard, Place

A city of southern Ontario, Canada, that is southwest of Toronto. It was named for the Mohawk leader Joseph Brant, who is buried nearby. Alexander Graham Bell performed some of his early experiments in sound transmission there in the 1870s.

Brantwood Drive

A longtime name of the surrounding area.

Brassell Alley, Street

The Brassells were once prominent Montgomery landowners.

Breckenridge Drive

John C. Breckenridge (along with Stephen A. Douglas) opposed Lincoln in the election of 1860 and received 18 percent of the vote.

Brentwood Drive

In an area of English-themed names. Brentwood is an area northeast of London.

Brevard Avenue

A town in the mountains of N. C. near the Nantahala National Forest. Some local developers had summer homes there.

Brewbaker Avenue

Cassie Leta Brewbaker was a local educator. Brewbaker schools are also named for her.

Brewer Court, Road

Named for its area, Brewer Heights, which was named for the family who owned much of the land north of U.S. 80 near Dannelly Field.

Brewton Street

A small town in S. Ala.

Briarbrook Drive

See Brookview Manor.

Briarcliff Road

A Montgomery contractor, Joe Sadler, thought this was a "good-sounding name." He said he "hated the story of Heathcliff [in *Wuthering Heights*] and used Briarcliff Road instead."

Briar Gate Court, Drive

In an eastern area once far from the central city, whose name was inspired by the brambles and briars formerly found in the rural setting.

Briar Glen Court

See Briar Gate Ct.

Briarhurst Drive

See Briar Gate Ct.

Briarwood Lane

See Briar Gate Ct.

Bridge Pointe

Crosses Jenkins Creek.

Bridle Path Court, Lane

See Carriage Hills.

Bridlewood Drive

Developer Aaron Aronov asked Joe Sadler, who was at that time a postal supervisor in charge of eliminating duplicate street names, and who became a contractor himself in the 1950s, to provide "good-sounding" names for the Normandale area. Sadler picked this one to call to mind the English of the landed gentry and their horsemanship.

Brighton Road

A borough of S.E. England located on the English Channel south of London which became a fashionable resort when royalty began to visit in the 18th century.

Brimwood Court

Near streets with tree names and references.

Brinsfield Drive

Sol E. Brinsfield, Jr., gave his name to the plat in this area when he served as attorney for the Industrial Board.

Bristol Court, Way

A port on River Avon in S.W. England.

Brittany Place

See Wynlakes.

Britton Lane

Prev. 6th St. and renamed for W.B. Britton and his four sons, veterans of WWII, who once occupied all of the houses on the street.

Broadview Street

Designates relatively high land, once thought to be healthier, in the Chisholm subdivision.

Broadway Street

A reference to the famous New York City theatre district.

Brockway Drive

For the glass company once located here. See Chisholm.

Bronner Road

Honors David Bronner, the current head of the Retirement Systems of Ala.

Brookgate Drive

See Brookview Manor.

Brookland Curve

See Wynbrook.

Brookline Lane

This street parallels Camp Creek.

Brooks Court, Road, Street

Prev. May Rd., this street was renamed to honor John Dallas Brooks, who owned a section of land in N.E. Montgomery. Upon his death, he left approximately 80 acres to each of his eight children. Many of his descendents built homes on the family place and the area became known as Brooksville by the early 20th century.

Brookstone Drive
See Wyndridge.

Brooktree Drive, Road
Dr.: See Brookview Manor. Rd: Close to White Slough, in a neighborhood of streets named for meadows and woods.

Brookview Drive, Court
In Brookview Manor.

■ BROOKVIEW MANOR
A neighborhood near the Alabama River, with numerous streets using "brook" as the first or last part of the name as well as family names and other references.

Brookwood Street (E.)
In an area between Hannon Slough and Baldwin Slough where several steets have "brook" as part of their name.

Broughton Street
In an older section of town and probably referring to a family or former owner.

Browning Drive
Part of Harness Hill, the area was developed using mostly a western theme.

Brown Springs Road
Named for the natural spring on the McLemore property that is located off the Atlanta Hwy. After leaving the town of Montgomery, it was the first stagecoach stop at which travelers could refresh themselves.

Brownwood Court, Lane
See Taylor Crossing.

Bryan Street
L.J. Bryan, property owner with Moses Brothers in the late 1800s. See Jackson Ferry Road.

Bryn Mawr Road
A town and college in Pa.

Buckboard Road
See Carriage Hills.

Buckingham Drive
Buckingham Palace, a residence of British kings and queens.

The palace has nearly 600 rooms. The street is located in an area of British-themed street names.

Buckram Oak Drive

See Taylor Crossing.

Buford Street

Active supporter for the development of Capitol Heights.

Bullard Street

Possibly for Robert Lee Bullard (1861-1947), a West Point graduate and WWI military leader, who was elected to the Alabama Hall of Fame.

Bullock Street

Possibly for the family of Col. Edward Courtney Bullock, a state senator who was selected to deliver the formal welcoming address to the newly elected Confederate president, Jefferson Davis. Also, an Ala. county that was organized in 1866 and named for the same man.

Burbank Court, Drive

Luther Burbank (1849-1926), an American horticulturist who developed the Burbank potato and the Shasta daisy along with other fruits, vegetables and flowers. He died April 11, 1926, with these last words: "I don't feel good."

Burge Court

Sam Burge, an area property owner.

Burgwyn Road †

Burkelaun Drive

Martha Burke Rouse Fitzpatrick, the daughter of area developer L.D. Rouse.

Burlington Drive

A city that is the home of the University of Vermont. Also, a city in N.C., a state where some local developers had summer homes.

Burns Street

Part of J.H. Shreve's subdivision in 1906. Possibly named for John Fielding Burns, delegate to the Alabama Constitutional Conventions of 1875 and 1901, state legislator and delegate to five Democratic National Conventions; or perhaps for Robert Benjamin Burns, a state senator in 1915.

Burnt Hickory Drive

In an area of streets named for trees.

Burton Avenue

The main street of the Burtonville subdivision located west of Cloverdale. It was owned by E.R. and Mary Holt in 1893.

Burtonway Drive †

Busch Street

Possibly for family of John William Busch (1841-1911), Alabama lawyer and president of Henderson Steel Co.

Bush Hill Road

Descriptive, generic.

Business Park Drive

A business district situated off the Troy Hwy.

Butler Avenue

Prev. Avenue E, located on Gunter Annex of Maxwell AFB, it now honors 2nd Lt. James H. Butler, the fifth American to die in an aircraft accident while stationed at Gunter Field. He was killed Nov. 29, 1941.

Byrne Drive

Byrne Jones, the wife of real estate developer Irby Jones.

C

Cabot Street

Cabot Land Co., a development company. See Highland Gardens.

Caddell Street †

Caffey Drive

D. Caffey, a real estate developer and owner of several diverse local businesses.

Cahaba Street

Cahaba, near Selma, was the capital of Alabama in the early 1800s until ravaged by disease and floods.

Cairnbrook Drive

For a member of Ida Bell Young's family.

Caldwell Court, Place

Probably for Herschell Caldwell, a popular coach at Lanier High School during the 1920s.

Calhoun Road, Street

For Calhoun County, organized in 1932 and named for the

fiery state's rights advocate John C. Calhoun.

California Street (N. & S.)
Honors the state of Calif.

Calloway Street
An active supporter for the development of Capitol Heights.

Calmar Drive
See Carriage Hills.

Cambridge Road
Honors Cambridge University in England.

Camden Street
Prev. Lee St., Pointer St., and Seventh St., it is one of a series of parallel downtown streets and perpendicular to Bell St. that are named for Alabama counties and towns starting with the letter "C."

Camellia Drive
The camellia is now the state flower of Alabama, adopted in 1954. See Golden Rod Ct.

Camelot Court
Seat of King Arthur's Court in the Arthurian legend. See "Wynton M. Blount Cultural Park."

Campbell Road
Colin Campbell, a friend of developer William K. Thames, Sr. See Woodley Rd.

Camp Creek Court
In an area with a western theme, such as Remington, Chaparral and Harness Hill.

Canna Drive
A variety of lily.

Cannon Street
Located on Maxwell AFB, the street honors Gen. John K. Cannon, a 1936 graduate of the Air Corps Tactical School; Chief of U.S. Military Mission, Argentina, in 1938; Chief of Staff 1st Air Force in 1940; Commander in Chief of all Allied Air Forces in the Mediterranean Theatre in 1945; Commanding General of USAF Europe in 1945.

Cannonball Drive
See Bell Station.

Canterbury Court, Drive
Location of the Episcopal church's apartments for senior citi-

zens. A reference to Canterbury, seat of the Church of England.

Canyon Court (E. & W.)
See Valley Rd.

Capitol Avenue
On a direct line to the capitol, the street runs perpendicular to N. and S. Capitol Pkwy. in Capitol Heights.

■ CAPITOL HEIGHTS
This neighborhood, developed around WWI, shows many patterns, including the names of states and untraceable surnames probably important in the development of the area.

Capitol Parkway (N. & S.)
Prev. Central St., now a main thoroughfare through Capitol Heights. The northern part was once Lasseter St.; the southern part was previously Hood St.

Capitol Plaza Drive
Located in Capitol Industrial Plaza and shopping center.

Capouano Drive
Leon Capouano, a Montgomery attorney and investor in Brighton Estates development.

Capri Street
An island off the coast of Italy that is noted for its popularity with tourists.

Capstone Court, Drive
Paul Corwin named this street after a University of Alabama landmark in a friendly rivalry with developer Ed Lowder, an Auburn University graduate who owned nearby property.

Capwood Court, Curve
A combining of the word "capitol" with the wood themes of the Montwood neighborhood.

Cardinal Lane
See Forest Hills subdivision. Colorful red birds, especially visible in Montgomery in the spring.

Carey Drive
One of a series of streets in the Lee High School area named by 1920s developers for women's and family names and natural features.

Cargill Court
Among several streets named for people.

Carlisle Street
Prev. LeGrand St. , possibly renamed for the family of Pompey Worthy Carlisle, a state legislator in 1915.

Carlo Street
In an area of first names used for streets.

Carlton Street
Possibly for the family of James Thomas Carlton, a state senator in 1919.

Carmel Drive
A northern Calif. resort and beach.

Carmichael Court (N.), Parkway, Place, Road, Way
Carmichael Rd., named for a city highway department employee and developed as a service road parallel to Interstate 85, inspired the naming of several adjacent shorter streets. Another source says the name is for Neva Kate Carmichael, "schoolmarm" brought from Newnan, Ga., to teach the 12 children of landowner Seth Johnson. She married Seth Johnson, Jr., one of her pupils.

Carmon Place †

Carol Court
In an area of first names used for streets

Carolina Court
Charleston, S. C., was the inspiration for the Charleston Court neighborhood.

Carol Villa Drive
The subdivision land owner Seth Johnson's daughter, Caroline.

Caroline Street
The wife of early Montgomerian Philemon Sayre. The name Caroline continued through two generations. See Virginia Ave.

Carriage Place
Reminiscent of 19th-century travel by buggy or chaise.

Carriage Barn Lane
See Carriage Hills.

Carriage Brook Road
See Carriage Hills.

■ CARRIAGE HILLS
Developed by John Bowman and C. Ray Amos. Mr. Amos

"tried to think of fun, catchy names," often with country associations.

Carriage Hills Court, Drive
See Carriage Hills.

Carriage Oaks Drive
In a neighborhood with country themes for streets, as in Coach, Lazy Brook and Horseshoe.

Carrie Street
See Capitol Heights.

Carter Hill Road
Begins on land once known as Carter's Hill on U.S. 231 S. and is thought to have been once owned by the Eugene Carter family. Today, Carter Hill Rd. takes a right-angle turn because at the time of Carter's Hill farm, property at the eastern side of that intersection blocked travel heading eastward and travelers had to head south for a distance.

Carver Street
George Washington Carver (1864-1943) was born to Mo. slave parents and rose to the position of director of the Department of Agricultural Research at Tuskegee Institute (1896-1943). He developed more than 100 different products from the peanut and the sweet potato including plastics, lubricants, ink, dyes, medicines, wood stains, face creams, tapioca and molasses. He was instrumental in shifting Southern agriculture from the exclusive planting of cotton.

Castlebrook Drive
See Brookview Manor.

Castle Ridge Road
In area with names evocative of an earlier era.

Cater Drive
In a neighborhood of streets named for people.

Catherine Drive †

Cathy Drive
In a neighborhood of streets named for people.

Catoma Street
The Indian name for a creek in Montgomery, derived from "oki" (water) and "tohoma" (a nearby Muskhogean tribe).

Cecil Lane
Cecil Lane once owned the property where this street is located.

Cedar Avenue, Place, Street
Ave: One of three parallel streets named for trees (Oak, Cedar and Elm) bisected by Orchard Avenue. One Cedar St. goes into Oak Park; another is located on Maxwell AFB.; a third goes to John M. Patterson State Vocational and Technical School. Cedar Pl. is in Garden Square. Also, one of the three telephone exchanges that existed in the city prior to 1941.

Cedar Ridge Court
In an area of Bellwood dotted with names of trees.

Cedarwood Lane
Descriptive, generic.

Cedric Court †

Ceiba Court
See Halcyon. Also, a silk cotton tree.

Celia Court
In a neighborhood of streets named for people.

Center Street (E. & S.)
Once situated between the two parallel North and South Streets, it was part of James B. Copeland's 1866 development, and is located west of what is now Interstate 65. South St. no longer exists there. See North St.

Center Drive
See Maxwell AFB.

Central Parkway (S.), Street
Pkwy.: When Ida Bell Young sold this property for development, she requested that this street be named Central Park Way and wanted a park to be located here. The street was named Central Parkway, and no park has been created. Central St. would have been about halfway from the heart of downtown to Fairview Ave. At the time, it marked the southern boundary of the city.

Central Railroad Street
Parallels the now-abandoned railroad tracks south of Clisby Park.

Chadburn Crossing

One of two steets to intersect with Taylor Rd. planned to start with "C" to go with "crossing." The city rejected the second one, now called Plantation Crossing.

Chalmers Court

See Sturbridge.

Chambers Place, Street

Prev. Second St., it now honors a N.E. Ala. county organized in 1832 and named for Sen. Henry Chambers of Ala.

Champion Street

See Highland Gardens.

Chancelor Court

Named by Tranum Fitzpatrick as a contraction for the Civil War battle of Chancellorsville.

Chandler Street

Reportedly named for Bill Chandler, a long-time executive secretary of the city's YMCAs. One of a series of downtown streets located in an industrial area near the Alabama River.

Chantilly Way

Located near the plantation of the same name on Vaughn Rd.

Chanute Street

Located on Maxwell AFB, the street honors Octave Chanute, a close friend of Orville and Wilbur Wright. During the second half of the 19th century, Chanute built and flew gliders, motorless aircraft that depended upon air currents for flight.

Chaparral Drive

In a western-themed area developed when *Bonanza* was a top-rated TV show.

Chapman Street

R.A. Chapman, a civil engineer and surveyor of this area.

Chappell Drive, Street

Joseph Chappell, the landowner in 1887.

Chappelle Lane

Possibly for a development in Mass.

Charingwood Court

Among a group of streets with "wood" as part of their names: Hollowwood, Blythewood, Saddlewood; near Forest Ridge.

Charles Street

One in a series of streets in north Montgomery (mostly private) with men's first names; another is in Capitol Heights, an area developed in the 1920s with family and individuals' names.

Charleston Court (N. & S.)

Honors Charleston, S. C.

Charleton Drive

Middle name of Paul Corwin, a local real estate developer.

Charlie Brassell Place

The president of Asphalt Contractors, Inc.

Charlotte Street

One of a number of city streets named for cities in N.C.

Charnwood Drive

Perhaps for "Charmwood," an English noble title.

Chartres Lane

A city of northern France southwest of Paris. Its 13th century cathedral is a masterpiece of Gothic architecture noted for its stained glass and asymmetrical spires.

Chase Street

Prev. Chandler St. See Capitol Heights.

Chateau Circle

A French manor house.

Chatham Place

A municipal borough of southeast England east of London. Elizabeth I established the first dockyard here in 1588.

Chatsworth Drive

The site in England of the conservatory that served as a model for the Crystal Palace, the architectural wonder at the London Exhibition of 1851.

Chattahoochee Drive

A river that forms the lower half of the boundary between Ala. and Ga. The name signifies "marked rocks," and is derived from the Creek "chato" (rocks) and "huchi" (marked).

Chatwood Street

An English-sounding name without any known place reference, in an area using "wood" as a suffix as well as other outdoor references.

Cheaha Court

For Cheaha Mountain, the highest point in Ala. It is located on the northern boundary of Clay County. A settlement of Chiaha Indians once existed among the Lower Creeks along the Chattahoochee and Flint Rivers. Cheaha may be derivative of the Choctaw "chaha" (high).

Cheekwood Lane

An English-sounding name without any known place reference, in an area of "-wood" and other outdoor references.

Chelsea Drive

See Chisholm.

Cheltenham Drive

An English resort city featuring mineral springs, popular since the early 1700s. Located in a neighborhood of streets named for places in Britain.

Chennault Circle

Lt. Gen. Claire L. Chennault, a pioneer aviator who gained renown initially as the leader of an aerial acrobatic team known as the "Men on the Flying Trapeze." In 1938 he reorganized the Chinese Nationalist Air Force at Mme. Chiang Kai-Shek's request. Then, with tacit approval from U.S. officials, he organized and led the Flying Tigers, a group of American volunteers in China flying American-made planes, who were credited with shooting down 250 Japanese aircraft between Dec. 1941 and July 1942.

Chenowith Lane

Relatives on the fraternal side of Ida Bell Young's family, who were dairy and cattle farmers on and beyond what is now the site of the Young Farm area.

Cherokee Drive

A tribe of North American Indians originally in the Alabama area and later removed by force to Okla. Also, for Cherokee County, organized in 1836.

Cherry Street

See Highland Park.

Cherry Creek Court, Drive

In an area featuring tree names for streets.

Cherry Hill Road

See Regency Park.

Cherry Tree Terrace
Ida Bell Young asked that cherry trees be planted on this street.
See Young Place.

Cherry Wood Trail
Near Old Orchard La.

Chesterfield Court
District and borough, county of Derbyshire, England.

Chestnut Street
Streets in Highland Park and on Maxwell AFB. Also, one of a
series of streets in the Lee High School area named by 1920s
developers for women's names, natural features and family
names.

Chevy Chase Drive
A 15th-century English ballad describing the Battle of
Otterburn between the Percys and the Douglases. A town in
Md. near Washington, D.C.

Chinaberry Court
In a neighborhood with botanical street names.

Chippewa Court
Woodland tribe of the Algonquin family; ranged both shores
of Lake Superior and Huron across Minn. to N.D.

Chipping Terrace
English-sounding name in English Village.

■ CHISHOLM
John Chisholm, the owner of the property on which the
Chisholm subdivision was developed.

Chisholm Street
See Chisholm.

Choctaw Drive, Street
Prev. Fourth St., it now honors the largest tribe of the southern branch of the Muskohegan family.

Christina Court †

Christy Lane
See Regency Park.

Chrystan Court, Road
Ct.: A short street off Chrystan Rd. in County Downs. Rd:
one in County Downs and one in Fox Hollow; it is planned
for the two to eventually connect.

Chuck Court †

Church Street
The location of Montgomery's first church. Union Church was built in the 1820s at the corner of Court St. and Church St. It was led by the Rev. Moses Andrews and Elder William Sayre and used by Methodists, Baptists and Presbyterians.

Churchill Drive
Near Westminster Presbyterian Church, recalling Winston Churchill's leadership of England during WWII. He died in 1965 at age 90. His last words were: "Oh, I am so bored with it all."

Citadel Street
The Citadel, a military college in S. C.. It was founded in 1842.

Citrus Street
In an area of tree-related street names.

Civitan Street
A civic organization founded in 1917 in Birmingham, Ala., to foster good citizenship.

Clanton Avenue
Possibly for Maj. Gen. James Holt Clanton (1827-1871), a Georgia-born lawyer who led a brigade formed in Montgomery during the Civil War. He was killed in an argument over one of his cases by an ex-Union colonel, David M. Nelson.

Clara Street
Clara E. Miller, wife of E.B. Miller and owner of property in Highland Gardens. The street was named by Highland Gardens developer Fred Cramton.

Claremont Avenue (E.)
See King's Hill.

Clarence Lee Drive †

Clarendon Road
See Halcyon.

Clarke Street
Part of W.D. Westcott's estate, Woodrow Place, in 1912. Possibly (misspelled) for planter Alexander Humphreys Clark, husband of Sallie McGehee Graves, granddaughter of Abner McGehee. See McGehee Rd. Also, possibly Clarke County, org. Dec. 10, 1812; named for Gen. John Clarke of Ga.

Clay Street

Clement Comer Clay, the first Ala. Supreme Court chief justice (1820-23) and former governor (1835-37).

Clayton Park, Street

Early Ala. family whose land, located W. of Court St., adjoined the Sayres' land. In 1818 George Root Clayton, along with several other investors, purchased the land that soon became "East Alabama."

Clearbrook Court

In an area of streets named for watercourses.

Clear Creek Court

In an area of streets named for watercourses.

Clearview Street

Parallel to Home View St.

Clebourne Street

Prev. Sixth St. A county in E. Ala. created in 1867 and named for Maj. Gen. Patrick R. Clebourne.

Clement Curve

First name of developer C. T. Fitzpatrick; the street was named by his wife.

Clemice Lane

See Heatherton Heights.

Cleve Drive

Among other streets using first or last names.

Cliff Road

Parallels Three Mile Creek.

Clint Court

For Clinton Thames, son of developer William K. Thames, Sr.

Clinton Street

Settlements in Greene County and Coffee County were named for the pioneering Clinton family.

Clio Street

The area was owned by J.C. Dale and J.H. Shreve in 1907. It was possibly named for the muse of history.

Clisby Park

Prev. Park Ave. John H. Clisby (1840-1902), cotton merchant, councilman, and mayor of Montgomery for two terms.

Clopton Street

Industrial leader David Clopton, former associate justice of the Ala. Supreme Court. Former member of the U.S. House of Representatives (1859-60). After secession, he resigned in favor of state politics. He died in 1892 and is buried in Oakwood Cemetery.

Cloud Street

Probably for Dr. Noah B. Cloud, a wealthy planter who worked for agricultural reform after moving to Ala. in 1838. He published the *American Cotton Planter* and in 1857 bought the *Montgomery Advertiser*. He fought for the South during the Civil War, but afterward became a Scalawag. His popularity declined sharply; he died in 1875.

Clover Court, Lane

In the heart of Cloverland.

■ CLOVERDALE

Cloverdale, the oldest garden-landscaped residential suburb in Alabama, was designed by the Olmstead brothers of a Boston architectural firm. Originally known as "Graham's Woods" (for the owner) and later referred to as "The Pines," the area was first developed by the Cloverdale Land and Development Co. in 1893. The Cloverdale name was inspired by the open glens of clover interspersed among the virgin pines. It was the second true streetcar suburb in Montgomery, after Highland Park. The initial development company declared bankruptcy in 1908 and reorganized as Cloverdale Homes. The houses then built were designed by such architects as Frank Lockwood, Sr., and Jr., B. B. Smith, Weatherly Carter and Nicholas Homes. Cloverdale was incorporated as a town on August 6, 1910. Clayton Tullis served as the town's first mayor. On Oct. 1, 1927, Cloverdale joined with Montgomery, and the annexation increased the city limits from less than seven square miles to more than twenty. Part of the annexation now known as the Garden District was added to the National Register of Historic Places in 1984.

Cloverdale Park (E. & W.)

Cloverdale Park of Cloverdale development. See "Cloverdale."

Cloverdale Road

Prev. Citheral Rd., Prairie St. Main thoroughfare of Cloverdale development. See "Cloverdale."

Clover Field Road

See Wynlakes.

Cloverhill Drive

In the heart of Cloverland.

Cloverlane Court

In the heart of Cloverland.

Clovis Drive

Possibly a family name. Of interest: Clovis united the Franks into one kingdom in the early Middle Ages. The name "Louis," taken by many French monarchs, is a version of his name.

Clower Street

See Highland Gardens.

Clubview Street

Near the site of the original Montgomery Country Club.

Coachman Road

See Carriage Hills.

Cobb Street

Rufus Willis Cobb, governor of Ala. (1878-82). Of interest: Howell Cobb was the speaker of the Ala. House of Representatives during the 1860s.

Cobbington Road †

Cobblestone Court

Parallel to Sandstone and Limestone courts. Cobblestones, known as "Belgium blocks," were brought to Ala. as ballast for ships coming from Europe for a load of cotton. Many of the city's streets, especially near the riverfront, were first paved with these stones, and in many cases asphalt now covers the original stones.

Coca-Cola Road

Leads to the local Coca-Cola bottling plant.

Cochran Circle

Carol Villa street probably named by developers who bought the land from the Johnson family.

Coffee Street

Prev. First St. S.E. Ala. county, organized in 1841 and named for Gen. John Coffee, surveyor general of the Ala. Territory. He surveyed the land that is now Montgomery. In 1813, Coffee and his troops burned and looted Black Warrior's town. One of Coffee's men, Davy Crockett, wrote about the event.

Colbert Street

Prev. Second St. N.E. Ala. county. The county was created in Feb. 1867, abolished a few months later and created again within two years. Named for Chiefs George and Levi Colbert of the Chickasaw nation.

Coleman Street

Pharaes Coleman, Cloverdale developer and major stockholder of the Electric Street Railway Co. in the early 1900s.

Colfax Drive

In a series of streets with names in alphabetical order from Ardmore to Esmond.

Colgate Drive

A university for men in Hamilton, N.Y., founded in 1819 and named for the William Colgate family (of Colgate-Palmolive), university benefactors, in 1890. See College Grove.

Coliseum Boulevard, Parkway

Location of Garrett Coliseum; see "Garrett Coliseum."

College Court, Street

Ct.: Developed by College Court Realty in 1911 (A.W. Dahlberg, president and treasurer; B.T. Dell, secretary). St.: Prev. Frederick St. In honor of Huntingdon College, originally the Methodist College for Women, which also inspired the College Pk. development, now known as East Cloverdale. See "Cloverdale" and Huntingdon Ct.

■ COLLEGE GROVE

Developers named the streets for colleges and universities in which they had an interest.

Colline Close, Drive

French for "hill"; combines some letters of names Paul Corwin and the family of Inge Hill, Sr., area developers.

Colonial Drive (N. & S.)

Named by developer C. T. Fitzpatrick; Alabama was colonized during its history by France, Spain and England.

Colony Street

Reference to Alabama's colonial past.

Columbia Street

Named by W. R. Westcott in 1893. "Columbia" was popularly used at this time to refer to the United States, as in "Hail, Columbia."

Columbus Street

Christopher Columbus (1451-1506), the Italian explorer credited with discovering the New World. He died in Valladolid, Spain, in 1506 at age 58, following numerous voyages. He once said: "The farther one goes, the more one learns."

Commerce Street

An early Montgomery business center, known as Main St. until 1825.

Commodore Circle, Street

Possibly for "Commodore" Cornelius Vanderbilt (1794-1877), American steamship and railroad operator, financier and major contributor to Vanderbilt University in Nashville, Tenn.

Community Street

Near Maxwell AFB, suggesting the base's relationship to the Montgomery city area.

Como Court

Mrs. L.D. Rouse loved Perry Como's music and named this street for him.

Computer Loop

The USAF moved its Communications Computer Programming Center to Gunter Air Force Station. This street is located on the military facility and runs in front of the Data Design Center.

Concord Mews

In an area of references to New England towns. "Mews" means stables grouped around a court or along a lane or alley.

Conecuh Street

Prev. Third St. A S. Ala. county organized in 1818 and named for the Conecuh River.

Cong. Wm. L. Dickinson Drive

Prev. Federal Dr. An Alabama Republican who served in the U.S. House of Representatives for 28 years. Given this honor in recognition of his service as Minority Chairman of the House Armed Services Committee. Renaming caused controversy among residents and led to the nickname "Cong Drive."

Congress Street

Probably for the legislative body of the U.S. and named during a period of enhanced patriotism.

Conlay Court

Named by W. Inge Hill, Jr.,—whose family once owned the land—for his imaginary childhood friend, Naughty Conlay, whom he blamed for misdeeds.

Conley Circle, Court

A city in Georgia.

Connie Circle

In a neighborhood of streets named for people.

Conrad Street †

Constantine Drive

The Roman emperor who converted the empire to Christianity after reportedly seeing a flaming cross in the air. He convened the Council of Nicea, and Constantinople was named in his honor.

Conti Lane †

Contractors Drive

Located north of Montgomery and Gunter industrial parks.

Cook Avenue

G. Arthur Cook, president of West Boylston Manufacturing Co. See Boylston St.

Cooke Street

Prev. Pike St. Grandmother of Robert Pinkston, developer of Capitol Heights.

Cookie Court

In an area of streets bearing first names.

Coosa Court, Street

The Coosa, uniting with the Tallapoosa River 11 miles below Wetumpka, forms the Alabama River. Probably derived from Choctaw "Kusha" (cane). Coosa County organized in 1832.

Coosada Drive

A creek in Elmore County; takes its name from an Upper Creek tribe of the Alabamoes known as the "Koasati."

Copperfield Court, Drive (N. & S.)

Routes into and across the Copperfield neighborhood.

Coral Lane

One of a few references to tropical plants and scenes in Seth Johnson Estates.

Corbett Street

John Corbett, an area property owner when the street was named in 1887.

Coretta Drive

For Coretta Scott King, the wife of the Rev. Martin Luther King, Jr. Situated near Luther Dr. See Luther Dr.

Cornell Road

A university in Ithaca, N.Y., founded in 1865. See College Grove.

Cornwall Court

One of a series of references to England and New England in the Fairfield neighborhood.

Cortez Street

Hernando Cortez (1485-1547), the Spanish explorer noted for his bloody conquest of Mexico.

Corwin Drive

Paul Corwin, Sr., an area real estate developer.

Cory Street

See Capitol Heights.

Cottage Place

Cottages and bungalows enjoyed popularity at the time of development of Cloverdale. See Cloverdale.

Cottingham Drive

W. A. Cottingham, chairman of the board and president of Alabama National Bank.

Cotton Court, Street

A staple plant of the South, and once the primary money crop of the area.

Cottondale Road

One of a series of streets in the Perry Hills subdivision ending with "dale." (See Avondale Rd., Beechdale Rd.)

Cottonwood Drive, Road

See Maxwell AFB and Forest Hills subdivision.

Council Street

Prev. Bryan St. Named by W.D. Westcott, a property owner in the western part of the city, in 1906.

Country Court

A country area before development of the bypass. Now an area of country-themed streets.

Country Brook Drive

In the same area as Country Ct.

Country Church Drive

Believed to have once been the site of a country church.

Country Club Drive (N.)

Located near Montgomery Country Club.

Countryside Lane

Still truly near the country in northeast Montgomery.

Countrywood Court

In an area with "wood"-themed streets.

County Court

In Interstate Industrial Park crossing the street named for Montgomery's Mayor Emory Folmar.

■ COUNTY DOWNS

Streets in County Downs were named by Pep Pilgreen after horse racing sites and terminology, as in Churchill Downs and the Kentucky Derby.

County Downs Court, Road

See County Downs.

Court Street (N. & S.)

Prev. Back St. Bitter rivalry still existed when East Alabama Town and New Philadelphia, the original towns in the downtown Montgomery area, merged. On Dec. 3, 1819, a legislative act settled the dispute over the location of the courthouse by designating the "Artesian Basin" as its permanent location. The street on which the basin was located was a neutral zone between the two towns. In 1960, city commissioners changed the name of Court Square to Confederate Square for one year in honor of the centennial of the Civil War. A controversy erupted in the early 1970s over the closing of a portion of Court St. between Dexter and Washington. A brick plaza covers the area.

Courtland Drive

In a neighborhood of streets named for people.

Courtney Drive

See "Montgomery's Own Philadelphia Story."

Coventry Road

Lady Godiva and her husband founded a Benedictine abbey in Coventry, England, in 1043. Site of a modern cathedral built to replace one that was destroyed during WWII.

Covered Bridge Drive
See Carriage Hills.

Covina Court †

Covington Street
Prev. Fourth St. S. Ala. county on the Fla. border organized in 1822 and named for Brig. Gen. Leonard W. Covington of Md.

Cox Lane
A family name important to the development of Garden Square.

Coyle Street †

Craig Street
Prev. Church St. For the family of Benjamin Hogan Craig, who was appointed as register of chancery (1863-68). He was the only Democratic officer retained during Reconstruction.

Cramer Avenue
Part of the Cramer family property on 1887 plat map.

Cramton Bowl

The city's only public football stadium, home field for Alabama State University and public high schools. Built on lands donated to the city specifically for this purpose by Fred J. Cramton, to whom they were returned when funds could not be raised. Cramton began construction of the stadium himself with his own crew of wagons and mules. Through his tireless efforts, $31,000 was raised to complete the stadium in 1921.

Crane Street
Possibly for William Crane, pastor of First Baptist Church in the 1830s.

Crawford Street
William O. Crawford, president of Southern United Life Insurance Co.

Creative Street

Prev. Traction Ave. Ann Morgan, a resident of the street, decided to change the name because there were two streets of this name. She wanted to use a family name, but all were already street names. As a cake decorator, she decided to be creative.

Creek Court, Drive

Common tribal name of the Muskogee Indians; settled in Ga. and Ala.

Crenshaw Court, Place

Prev. Fifth St. Anderson Crenshaw (1785-1847), originally from S. C., was appointed to the Alabama Supreme Court in 1821 and as circuit judge from 1832-38. Or, the S. Ala. county organized in 1866 and named for the same judge.

Crescent Road

Descriptive of its course.

Cresta Circle

In a neighborhood of streets named for people.

Crest Hill Drive

Descriptive, generic.

Crestmont Drive

An entrance to Woodcrest.

Crestview Avenue

For the view of Bonnie Crest Country Club.

Cricklewood Drive

In an area of streets with woods or wood themes.

Cromer Drive

In a series of streets named for people.

Cromwell Street

Prev. Hubbard St., Noble St. Possibly for Oliver Cromwell (1599-1658), one of the dominant figures of the Puritan movement proclaimed "protector" and ruler of Great Britain. When the monarchy was restored, his body was taken from its tomb at Westminster Abbey and hanged.

Croom Drive

Laura Sarah Croom, wife of local landowner Leonidas Hill.

Cross Bend Court

Descriptive of the street's curve.

Crossbow Drive

Carol Villa street probably named by developers later than the Johnson family, original landowners.

Cross Creek Court, Drive

In Cross Creek neighborhood. Drive would cross Baldwin Slough if it continued north.

Crossgate Trail

In a recently rural area where farmland fences once required gates.

Cross Ridge Road

Close to Baldwin Slough in a neighborhood between it and Whites Slough.

Crossway Drive

Crosses Mobile Hwy.

Crouson Street

See Highland Gardens.

Croydon Road

A district in southeastern England.

Crumpton Drive †

Crystal Road †

Cullen Street

In a neighborhood of streets named for people.

Cullman Street

Prev. Sixth St. N. Ala. county and city. County organized in 1877 and named for Johann G. Cullman.

Cumberland Road

For Cumberland Gap, in mountains of that name, a southwestern branch of the Appalachians.

Cunningham Drive

In a neighborhood of several streets named for people.

Cypress Court (E. & W.), Lane

In a neighborhood with botanical street names, especially trees.

D

D Street

D, E and F streets are short parallels connecting Blackburn Ave. to Ripley St.

Dabney Avenue

Possibly named for Dr. G. W. Dabney, a noted physician who moved to this area from Va. in the early 1800s.

Dagger Hole Road

A nearby night club sold Dagger wine. Residents have recently changed the street to Sanders La., honoring Annie and Henry Sanders, who were longtime area landowners.

Daisy Court, Ridge

Wildflower common to this area; in a neighborhood with botanical names.

Dale Drive

J.C. Dale, the owner of a development in the early 1900s. Of note: Dale County was organized in 1824 and named for Gen. Sam Dale. In 1818, Gen. Dale established Ft. Dale on the Old Federal Rd. north of Greenville to provide protection from Savannah Jack and his band of hostile Indians.

Dalford Drive †

Dallas Drive

A developer sought "good-sounding names" for this area and checked out-of-town city directories. Folklore has it that Dallas, Texas, was named for a mule that died there when it was a mere stagecoach stop. Dallas County was named for A.J. Dallas, former U.S. secretary of the treasury.

Dalphon Road

A Carol Villa street that was probably named by later developers than the Johnson family, original landowners.

Dalraida Court, Parkway, Place, Road, Terrace

Named by George Laurie for the small community of Dalriada (street misspelled) near Edinburgh, Scotland. He purchased the land from a member of the Ware family in 1909. See "The Dalraida Neighborhood."

Daman Drive

A region of N.W. India on the eastern shore of the Gulf of Cambay.

The Dalraida Neighborhood

The name "Dalriada" refers to ancient kingdoms in both Scotland and Ireland. It is the name of an ancient Irish ruler and means "race of Riada." Some of Riada's people crossed over to Britain in 506 A.D. Around 575 A.D., after years of strife, some of the Dalriadans, under King Adan, broke away from the Irish Dalriadans and settled in Scotland.

Who brought the name to Montgomery and who changed the spelling? The original 1827 deed to the area shows the name as "Dalriada." In 1911, *The Alabama Journal* used the same spelling in an article about George Laurie, who had purchased the property from Elizabeth Alabama (Ware) Lyman in 1909. Laurie was born in the small community of Dalriada, near Edinburgh, Scotland.

In platting the land, the name stayed "Dalriada," but over the years a clerk or perhaps a sign painter transposed the vowels and "Dalraida" began to appear on street signs and maps. That version is now firmly implanted on recent deeds and residents' minds.

Danbury Circle

See Regency Park.

Dane Drive †

Dannelly Court, Drive, Street

St.: Located on Maxwell AFB, the street memorializes Ensign Clarence Moore Dannelly, Jr., killed Dec. 17, 1940. Ct., Dr.: located in a neighborhood directly across from Dannelly Field, the municipal airport that was also named for Ensign Dannelly.

Danville Street

In an area with "Dan" in names for Dannelly Field. Danville is also a city in Va.

Daphne Court, Lane

In an area of women's first names used for streets, such as Ada, Glenda and Donna.

Darien Drive

City in Conn. Also, a Caribbean area between Panama and Colombia.

Darrington Road †

Dartmouth Circle

Dartmouth College, located in Hanover, N.H.

Davenport Drive

City in Iowa. Located among a series of streets with names in alphabetical order from Ardmore to Esmond.

David Drive

In a neighborhood composed of several streets named for people.

Davidson Street

Early prominent corn-broker family. Dr. Arlie B. Davidson taught sociology classes at Huntingdon College from 1938 to 1969. In addition, he wrote a daily column for the *Montgomery Advertiser* from 1942 until 1978.

Davis Drive, Street

Horace Davis, Sr., who took pride in building low-cost homes for veterans, which in the 1950s were the best bargains in Montgomery. He was the first to place a disappearing attic stairway in these homes.

Davors Drive

Dave and Orson Alexander, the fifth and seventh children (out of 12) of Seth Johnson, the former landowner of the Carol Villa area.

Dawn Drive

Descriptive, generic.

Day Street, Day Street Road

1878 *City Directory and History of Montgomery, Alabama* lists Ellen Day as a resident. No other Day family members have been located. Of note: Clarence Day, author of *Life With Father*, died in New York in 1935 about the time this street was named.

Debby Drive

Debby Pouncey, granddaughter of Geraldine LeCroy, who

owned the land on which LeCroy Shopping Center was developed.

Decatur Street (N. & S.)

War of 1812 Naval Commodore Stephen Decatur (1779-1820), who with a small crew fought Barbary pirates at Tripoli Harbor. They recaptured and blew up the American warship *The Philadelphia*, which the pirates had captured. Decatur's famous quote: "My country, right or wrong."

Dee Drive

Dee Rea, grandson of builder-developer-Realtor Shan Sellers. This is the only member of his family for whom he named a street in his many developments.

Deerfield Court, Drive

The signature street for its neighborhood.

Deer Trail Road

See Arrowhead West.

Delano Avenue

Franklin Delano Roosevelt (1882-1945), 32nd president of the U.S.

Delaware Street

The first state to ratify the U.S. Constitution (1787) and birthplace of John Falconer, one of the city's founders. State named in honor of Thomas West, Baron de la Warr, the first governor of Virginia, 1609-18. Early American settlers also gave the name to North American Indians who called themselves Lenni-Lenape.

Delfern Drive

Combination of "dell" and "fern" in Woodley Meadows.

Delwood Court

English-sounding name in English Village.

Delmar Drive

City in New York.

Delray Court, Road

Delray Beach, Fla.

Deming Street

In a neighborhood of streets named for people.

Dempsey Street

Jack Dempsey, world heavyweight champion, visited the city in 1930. His famous fight with Gene Tunney in 1927 excited one fan so much he stabbed himself with an icepick and died.

Dena Court
Carol Villa street probably named by later developers than the Johnson family, original landowners.

Denham Court
In an area of New England and English names.

Dennis Avenue
One of three parallel streets with family names.

Denton Drive
A city in Texas.

Derby Lane
See County Downs.

Dericote Street
In a neighborhood of steets named for people.

Derril Drive
In a neighborhood of streets named for people.

De Soto Street
Hernando De Soto, the Spanish explorer who is credited with the discovery of the Mississippi River. He passed through the village of Ecunchati (red ground or bluff) on Sept. 6, 1540. Montgomery now occupies the site of that village.

Destin Street
A N.W. Fla. city.

Devon Court
Carol Villa street probably named by later developers than the Johnson family, who were the original landowners.

Devonshire Drive
A county of S.W. England noted for clotted cream. In an English-themed neighborhood.

Dewanee Street
One of a series of streets in the Lee High School area named by 1920s developers for women's names, natural features and family names.

Dewey Street †
Of note: Thomas E. Dewey ran unsuccessfully for president twice. While running against F. D. Roosevelt in 1944, he made a discovery that could have cost FDR the race. General George Marshall, however, convinced him not to disclose to the public FDR's knowledge of the broken Japanese code

which led Dewey to believe that he had allowed the attack on Pearl Harbor in order to get the U. S. into the war.

Dexter Avenue

Prev. Market St., now honors Andrew Dexter, founder of New Philadelphia, which merged with East Alabama Town to form Montgomery. Another theory is that it was named for a street in Boston or Philadelphia, where Dexter had lived. Montgomery City Directory (1880-81) shows it as Market St.; the 1887 directory shows Dexter Ave. When this was Market St. in New Philadelphia, the Vickers family (see Van Allen Rd.) kept a tavern there. See "Andrew Dexter's Double Life."

Diane Court †

Dianne Lane †

Dickerson Street

Early Montgomery family who dealt in furniture and household goods.

Dillard Street

Owned by Chandler and Douglas in 1893, possibly named for family of James Richard Dillard, state legislator in late 1800s.

Dilworth Court, Road †

Division Street

A street which divides a flood plain peninsula in a bend of the Alabama River in the northwest section of the city.

Dixie Drive, Street

Ala. is known as the Heart of Dixie. Of interest: Dixie Bibb Graves, wife of Ala. Gov. Bibb Graves, was appointed to the U.S. Senate in August 1937 to fill Hugo L. Black's seat, vacated by his appointment to the U.S. Supreme Court. She was the first woman to represent Ala. in the U.S. Senate. See "The Heart of Dixie."

Dixon Street

While commanding the Confederate vessel *Fish*, George Dixon sank the Union ship *Housatonic*. Both ships sank; no lives were saved. Of interest: Frank M. Dixon was governor of Ala. (1939-43).

Dobbs Circle, Drive

In a neighborhood of streets named for people.

Andrew Dexter's Double Life

People think of Andrew Dexter as a man with a vision or, perhaps, as a gambling man. He was, after all, an attorney from Rhode Island who purchased a tract of land in Alabama before he ever saw it. Even the residents of New Philadelphia, the village he developed on his property, called him "an impetuous speculator" or "dexterous Dexter," giving him the credit for envisioning the capitol of Alabama on what was then pasture land called "Goat Hill."

However, there is a darker side of Andrew Dexter that few people know. According to some sources, he was a swindler and a fraud.

After graduating from Brown University, Dexter decided to follow in his father's footsteps and become a banker. He even tried his skill at real estate, but his enormous losses and eventual bankruptcy in that business convinced him to stick to banking. In 1808, he acquired the Farmers' Exchange Bank of Rhode Island and began generating bank notes that could be used as money in exchange for goods and services or could be exchanged for gold and silver at the bank. But Dexter printed more notes than he could back with gold and silver. So he instructed his employees to discourage the bank customers from redeeming their notes. This tactic soon led to a lawsuit and closure of the bank for lack of funds. When the bank was closed, the total value of notes held by patrons was $580,000 against gold and silver in the vault worth $86.48. The loss was huge for that time.

Despite the con man in Dexter's character, he is best remembered for his generosity. He set aside part of his land for a capitol building in hope that the town would someday become the center of state government, and he provided a portion of his land to be used as a burial ground for the townspeople. Ironically, he did not live to see the capitol relocated, nor was he buried in his cemetery. Around 1834, Dexter traded his remaining land for supplies and set out for Texas. He made it as far as Mobile and died during a yellow fever epidemic in 1837. He was buried there in an unmarked grave.

The Heart of Dixie

Anyone who hears the word "Dixie" thinks immediately of the South or the song of the same name.

The term for the area was probably taken from currency printed by the Citizens Bank and Trust Company of New Orleans. Because of the large number of French-speaking inhabitants in the area, the bills were printed in both English and French. The most commonly used denomination was $10, also known as "Dix," the French word for "ten." Traders in the 1830's began referring to the bills as "Dixies" and subsequently the area around the Mississippi River as "Dixie Land."

The song, composed in 1860 by Dan Emmett in New York, became popular in Montgomery after he performed the song in the Old Montgomery Theater on his tour of the South that year. In 1861, the song was performed for Stephen Douglas, who campaigned in Montgomery in his bid for the presidency of the United States against Abraham Lincoln. "Dixie" became the war song of the Confederacy at the inauguration of Jefferson Davis in Montgomery in 1863.

Dogwood Court, Drive, Lane, Street

Eastern Forest subdivision streets are named for the multitude of dogwood trees in the area. Bearing a profusion of white or pink flowers in early spring, the dogwood tree is common to the area. It heralds the end of winter and the coming of spring for Montgomery's residents.

Don Juan Court

A legendary Spanish nobleman who is famous for his amorous pursuit of the fairer sex. In a 1981 newspaper article, Joe Azbell refers to a "Don Wan Lane," but no such street exists today.

Donaldson Street †

Donna Drive
In a neighborhood of streets with women's first names.

Donovan Drive †

Dorchester Drive
English city, the model for Casterbridge in Thomas Hardy's novels. In an English-themed neighborhood.

Doris Circle, Street
In a neighborhood of streets named for people.

Dorothy Street
Named by W.D. Westcott in 1906.

Dosford Road †

Dothan Street
A S.E. Ala. city.

Douglas Street
Property owner with Chandler in 1893.

Dover Drive
See Regency Park.

Dovewood Court
See Mosswood. The Montgomery area, when more rural, was noted for excellent dove-hunting areas.

Dowell Lane †

Drake Street
In a neighborhood of streets named for people.

Drayton Lane
A suburb of Pontiac, Mich.

Dresden Court, Drive
German city where china is manufactured. It was heavily bombed in WWII and later extensively rebuilt.

Drexel Road
Among streets named for people.

Drivers Row
In an industrial area. Probably in honor of area truck drivers.

Druid Hills Drive
In the Druid Hills neighborhood.

Dubuque Drive
In an area of streets named for cities.

Duckworth Drive
For the Duckworth family, who were also related to the Nicrosi family.

Dudley Street
In a neighborhood of streets named for people.

Duff Street †

Dumas Street
French author Alexander Dumas, author of *The Three Musketeers* , *The Count of Monte Cristo*, and other classic works.

Dumont Drive
See Forest Hills.

Dunbar Street
A prominent landowning Montgomery family.

Dunbarton Road †

Duncan Circle, Drive
Cir: located on Gunter Annex of Maxwell AFB, probably named to honor Corp. Lawrence A. Duncan, who was killed in an air crash in 1934. Dr.: for Duncan Liles, a Montgomery developer and contractor.

Dundale Road
One of a series of streets in the Perry Hills subdivision ending with "dale," such as Cottondale and Elmdale.

Dunleith
See Wynlakes.

Dunn Drive
David Earl Dunn was mayor of Montgomery from 1944-46. James Dunn was a developer of Montgomery suburban areas.

Dunwoody Court, Lane, Place
See Wynlakes.

Dupont Street
A Delaware family, active in American Revolution, who later founded the Du Pont du Nemours Co. and became major philanthropists.

Duquesne Drive
In an area with streets named for French heroes and explorers. See "Montgomery's Own Philadelphia Story."

Durham Drive

One of a group of streets named for N.C. cities. See "Montgomery's Own Philadelphia Story."

Durward Drive †

Du Val Drive

See "Montgomery's Own Philadelphia Story."

Dyas Court, Drive

A developer for Brookview Manor.

E

E Street

One of three parallel lettered streets (D, E, F) linking Blackburn Ave. to Ripley St.

Eagerton Road

Col. Billy Eagerton and his wife, Edna, own a large farm in the area.

Eagle Road

In an area of avian names, such as Swan and Warbler.

Eagle Pass Road

Located in the hilly Mountain View Estates.

Eaker Street

Prev. 4th St. Located on Maxwell Air Force Base, renamed to honor Gen. Ira C. Eaker, a 1935 graduate of the Air Corps Tactical School. He piloted one of the planes on the Pan-American Goodwill trip to South and Central America in 1926-27. He was chief pilot on the "Question Mark" in 1929; Commanding General of the 8th Air Force in 1942; Commander-in-Chief of the Mediterranean Air Forces in 1944; Deputy Commanding General of AAF; and Chief of the Air Staff in 1945. He died Aug. 6, 1987.

Earl Place

Possibly for name of a civil engineer used frequently on plat maps in the late 1800s or for the first name of E.W. Clapp, property owner in 1880s.

Early Street

Jubal Early, a CSA general whose forces threatened Washington, D.C., in 1864.

East Drive, Street

Dr.: Inside Maxwell AFB, east of the main gate. The entrance to the AUM campus from Taylor Rd. St.: Two streets with the same name (one possibly a continuation of the other) in the Chisolm-Highland Gardens area; the easternmost streets in the Johnson plat.

Eastdale Circle, Drive, Loop, Road (S.)

Adjacent to Eastdale Mall.

Eastern Boulevard

The eastern leg of the perimeter route originally intended to bypass the city.

Eastern Ridge Court

Eastern street in a neighborhood of streets with "view" in the names.

Easthaven Road

See Forest Hills.

Eastmont Drive

In an area including a shopping center that in the 1960s would have been at the eastern edge of the city (i.e., a combination of "east" and "Montgomery").

East Patrick Court

In an area of last names used for streets.

Eastwood Glen Drive, Place

In a wooded area on the east side of the city.

East Virginia Lane

Numerous settlers from Va. came to populate the Alabama territory.

East Washington Street

Near Washington Ave., also in honor of George Washington.

Eddins Road

Liston Eddins, a local Realtor.

Edgar Street

See Capitol Heights.

Edgefield Road

In an area that, like many Montgomery neighborhoods, was originally farmland.

Edge Hill Lane

For the local landscape.

Edgemont Avenue (W.)
What was the southern edge of Montgomery at the time the street was named.

Edgeworth Drive
May have been named for Edgeworthstown, Ireland.

Edinburgh Court, Drive, Place
In a neighborhood with other Scottish associations.

Edward Street
Probably a family name important to the development of Garden Square.

Eighth Street
Sixth, Eighth and Ninth streets crisscross a riverside industrial area.

Eisenhower Drive
Dwight D. Eisenhower, supreme allied commander in WWII and 34th president of the U.S. (1952-60). The famous "Ike" died at age 78 in 1969 with these last words: "I've always loved my country."

Elaine Drive
Elaine Dunn, wife of developer James Dunn.

Elder Street
In a neighborhood of last names used for streets.

Eldington Drive
L.D. Rouse Fitzpatrick, son of Mr. and Mrs. C. T. Fitzpatrick, used his initials and added "ington" to them.

Elebash Hill
Camille Elebash-Hill, wife of W. Inge Hill, Jr., whose family once owned the land.

Eley Court
Jack Eley, First Alabama Bank vice president in the real estate division.

Eliza Court
A new street in the Bellehurst subdivision; probably a Larkin family name. The Larkin family once owned land in the Bellehurst area.

Elizabeth Street
Elizabeth Whetstone Thames, the wife of developer William K. Thames, Sr.

Ellen Street

The daughter of A. W. LeBron, developer of Cloverdale. See "Cloverdale."

Elliott Street

Probably for Collins D. Elliott, Huntingdon College president from 1864-65.

Ellis Drive

Among several streets named for people.

Ellsworth Drive

See Regency Park.

Elm Avenue, Street

Ave: One of three parallel streets named for trees (Oak, Cedar and Elm) bisected by Orchard Ave. St: Three different locations in the city (Highland Park, Maxwell AFB and downtown).

Elmdale Road

One of a series of streets in the Perry Hills subdivision ending with "dale," such as Beechdale and Forestdale.

Elmwood Street

Named in 1890s as part of the McVeigh and Boddes subdivision of the Stringfellow property.

El Paso Court, Street

A Texas city.

Elsberry Drive

Name of the developer of Elsberry Estates.

Elsmeade Drive

Another variant of Elsberry, the developer of this area.

Embee Drive

Suggestive of initials, in a neighborhood with streets using people's first names.

Emory Folmar Boulevard

Montgomery's mayor, 1977-present.

Empire Court, Road, Terrace

Empire Subdivision Co., a developer in the area.

Endicott Drive †

Endover Drive

Connects two streets, Bolton Dr. and Fleming Rd., all of which are probably named for local people.

Enfield Mews
See Halcyon.

English Oak Court, Loop
See Halcyon.

Enslen Street
Part of area developed by the Enslen family in 1893.

Erato Street
Was subdivided incorrectly and named because of the error, even then misspelled from *erratum* (singular) or *errata* (plural).

Eric Lane
See Regency Park.

Erskine Street
Possibly for Albert Russell Erskine (1871-1933), native of Huntsville who served as vice president of the Underwood Typewriter Co., president of Studebaker Corp., and president and chairman of the Board of Arrow Motor Car Co. He contributed financially to the state, but later committed suicide after losses in the Depression.

Erwin Drive
Probably a family name that is important to the development of Garden Square.

Esco Drive
Perhaps for Southlawn Co. (or Corp.), the developer of this residential area.

Esmond Road
In an area of streets with names in alphabetical order from Ardmore to Esmond.

Essex Place
In an area of English-themed street names. Essex was rumored to be a lover of Elizabeth I.

Estate Avenue
An entrance to Prairie View Estates.

Ester Street
In an area of several feminine names.

Eton Road
Honors England's prestigious Eton College, established in 1440 and located in Windsor near London.

Euclid Circle

Possibly for the third-century Greek mathematician. The geometry of the circle was part of his deductive principles of logic.

Eufaula Court

Town on the W. bank of the Chattahoochee in Barbour County; the center of a number of Creek settlements, one of which was near the present town.

Eugene Street

In an area of first and last names used for streets.

Eva Street

One of several downtown streets named for women and located in an industrial area near the Alabama River and a railroad.

Evans Drive

Mount Meigs was first known as Evansville for Jesse Evans who owned a tavern there. There is historical evidence that he later moved to town and became a fire fighter of some renown.

Everest Court, Drive

For Dr. Paul Everest, Montgomery orthopedic surgeon, who won the street-naming rights at an auction.

Evelyn Drive †

Ewell Street

Possibly related to a settlement in Dale County named by its first postmaster, Dallas Windham, for his son Ewell.

Excelsior Drive

Used with the meaning to strive ever harder and higher through adversity.

Exchange Street

The Exchange Hotel was a landmark of city hospitality. Area residents were able to purchase its woodwork and artifacts when it was demolished.

Executive Park Drive

The road that leads into the Executive Park office area.

F

F Street

One of three short parallel streets (D, E, F) linking Blackburn Ave. to Ripley St.

F. Scott Drive

For F. Scott Fitzgerald, who was stationed at Camp Sheridan during WWI, where he met and later married Montgomerian Zelda Sayre. He died in Los Angeles on Dec. 21, 1940, at age 44 in the home of Shelia Graham. See Fitzgerald Rd.

Fabel (also -Fable) Court

J. and Anna Fabel, who were area property owners in 1940s.

Fain Court

The C. L. Fain family owned acreage and was involved in the development of this area off Perry Hill Rd.

Fairfax Court, Road

See "Montgomery's Own Philadelphia Story."

Fairfield Court

See "Montgomery's Own Philadelphia Story." Cities in Australia, Conn., Calif. and Ohio, among others, also bear this name.

Fairforest Drive

In Olde Acres with other tree- and outdoor-themed names.

Fairground Road

Prev. Upper Wetumpka Rd. Changed in the early 1950s when Garrett Coliseum was constructed and the grounds were used for state fairs.

Fairlane Court, Drive

Descriptive, generic.

Fairlee Court

In an area of last and first names used for streets.

Fairmont Road

The "fair Montgomery." See Edgemont, Southmont, Eastmont, Alamont.

Fair Oaks Court, Drive

An area near Richmond, Va., where Confederates were defeated by Union forces in 1862. Near Willow Oaks.

Fairview Avenue

Fairview Plantation, named by John Jindrat and acquired in

1851 by Peter Mastin and his wife, Mary Myrick, sat south of what is now Fairview Ave. Probably a street marking the southern boundary of city development before the 1920s. The end of the trolley line in the early '20s was on Fairview Ave. in front of Huntingdon College near the current country club.

Fairway & Court
Located near the golf course at the Colonial Acres Country Club and the Standard Club.

Fairwest Place, Street
A curve that becomes Caffey Dr. where Fairview Ave. bends south to become the Mobile Hwy. in western Montgomery.

Fairwood Drive
Located in Woodley Meadows with Brooktree Rd., Meadowbriar Ct. and similar outdoor names.

Falcon Lane
A hawk-like bird whose range includes the Montgomery area. Also refers to a small cannon.

Falcon Ridge Court
In an area owned by the Tankersleys and Hills, a name that suggests its rural state before the development of nearby highways and mall.

Fallowfield Road
Much of Montgomery was once farmland that was rotated to improve crop production. Fields were allowed to remain fallow on alternating years to give them a "rest."

Fannin Road
Fred Fannin owned a popular men's clothing store in downtown Montgomery. It was mobbed one day by local people in the early 1940s when Clark Gable, then a cadet at Eglin Field, came to the store to be fitted for uniforms.

Farmfield Lane
Once Norris family farm holdings, now Norris Farms neighborhood.

Farmington Road
See "Montgomery's Own Philadelphia Story." A reference to the years of use for crops of much land now included in Montgomery's eastern suburbs.

Farnsworth Court
A developer said he named it for a favorite actor, Robert Farnsworth.

The Forgotten Founder

When Andrew Dexter made a 5 percent deposit on the land that was later to become Montgomery, he had severely depleted his funds. He soon met John Falconer, a wealthy merchant, who agreed to join Dexter in his new enterprise. Falconer paid for the quarter section selected as the site of the future town. Dexter's finances never seemed to improve; New Philadelphia and Falconer, however, flourished.

Falconer, born in 1776 at Smyrna, Del., was orphaned when young and apprenticed to a cabinet maker. Later he made his way to Manchester, S.C., and became a successful merchant. In 1817, he joined Andrew Dexter in his New Philadelphia investment and eventually opened a store on Market St. Falconer and his brother Joshua operated the store until 1830.

Falconer was a member of the city's Masonic fraternity and was also the city's first postmaster. On July 1, 1834, he bestowed his postal duties upon Neal Blue and became a planter. Eleven years later, the aging bachelor sold his land and slaves and lived with relatives until his death June 30, 1854, at the home of his sister-in-law, Mrs. William Falconer.

John Scott and Andrew Dexter are given joint credit as founders of the city. Dexter's silent partner is often forgotten. No known street exists today that is named in Falconer's honor.

Faro Court, Drive

A card game in which the players make bets on the top card of the dealer's pack.

Farrar Street

In a neighborhood of streets named for people.

Farrington Drive

Among several streets named for people.

Farwood Drive

One of a series of streets in the Perry Hills subdivision ending with "wood," such as Glenwood Rd. and Lakewood Dr.

Faunsdale Drive

Located in Dalraida, the street's name is suggestive of its wooded areas.

Federal Drive

Prev. Saffold Dr. Jimmy Heustess, a member of the Montgomery County Board of Commissioners, renamed it Federal Dr. after WWII when the national government federalized the municipal airport to create Gunter AFB. A portion of U.S. Hwy 231 N. that passes in front of Gunter Annex of Maxwell AFB was recently renamed for Congressman William L. Dickinson.

Felder Avenue

For the family of Adam Christopher Felder (1819-1880), an Ala. senator, and his nephew Richard Felder, a Montgomery public official and land developer.

Felder Terrace

Prev. St. Clair Ter. Reportedly changed at the request of its residents before WWII from St. Clair to Felder because it shared a name with a notorious "woman of the evening."

Fendall Hall Circle, Court

See Wynlakes.

Ferguson Street

Prev. Hannon Ave. Situated in a neighborhood of streets named for people.

Ferndale Court

Like "Faunsdale" and other words for street names created to suggest rural beauty, peace and wildlife.

Fernway Circle, Court, Drive

See Ferndale Ct.

Fernwood Drive

See Ferndale Ct.

Ferry Way

See Wares Ferry Rd.

Festival Drive

Location of the Ala. Shakespeare Festival. See "Wynton M. Blount Cultural Park."

Fieldbrook Court, Drive

Another compound descriptive name.

Fieldcrest Court,Drive

Developed and named by C.T. Fitzpatrick for the crest of the field.

Fieldstone Court

This area had stony fields when cultivated on the McLemore plantation. The McLemore family sold adjacent land to be used for the Auburn University at Montgomery campus.

Fifth Street

A series from First through Seventh intersecting Mobile Hwy.; also (& E. & W.). in Forest/Oak Park.

Finley Avenue, Curve

John Finley and his wife owned this area when it was called Finley Heights in 1897.

First Street

A popular street name, even when its numbered partners don't go past two or three. A series from First through Seventh intersecting Mobile Hwy.; another series from First through Seventh intersecting Lower Wetumpka Rd.; first in a short group of numbered streets intersecting Bell St. after the series of streets named for Ala. counties; short street linking Reese's Ferry with Birmingham Hwy. (Numbered streets have been omitted from this book unless they have unusual stories.)

First Alabama Plaza

A street connecting Dexter Ave. and Commerce St., where, because of the controversy surrounding the removal of the lions' head decorations from the historic First Alabama Bank Building, a plaza park was created in which some of the heads were mounted on a pedestal.

Fisher Road

Gunter Annex of Maxwell AFB, honoring Sgt. George H. Fisher, an ace parachutist and aerial photographer who achieved fame by his death-defying jump into Cramton Bowl in the 1930s.

Fisk Road †

Fitzgerald Circle, Road

F. Scott Fitzgerald, the author of novels including *The Great Gatsby* and *Tender is the Night*, and his wife, Zelda Sayre Fitzgerald, a Montgomery native. See Sayre St. and F. Scott Dr.

Fitzpatrick Avenue, Boulevard

Montgomery developer C. T. Fitzpatrick. The Fitzpatrick Elementary School is located on Fitzpatrick Blvd. Of interest: Benjamin Fitzpatrick was governor of Ala. from 1841-45 and a three-time U.S. senator. He is buried in Oakwood Cemetery.

Flack Road

Hunter Flack, a local lumberman.

Flair Drive

A name probably chosen in an effort to promote this area. See also Brookview Manor.

Flamingo Lane

A pink tropical bird. Located in an area with tropical references.

Fleming Road

Of interest: Prior to WWI, Dave Fleming owned and operated Fleming's Restaurant on Monroe St. The elegant dining facility was frequented by affluent diners from all over the Southeast around the turn of the century. See Bolton Dr. and Endover Dr.

Flint Street

See Capitol Heights.

Flintstone Court

A hard quartz stone that produces a spark when struck and was often used to start fires by Indians and pioneers. See Highland Gardens.

Flood Street

Named by W.C. Jackson, property owner in 1890s.

Floral Lane

See Pecan Grove Estates.

Florence Court, Street
In an area with other first names used for streets.

Florida Street (N. & S.)
Honors the state of Fla.

Flowers Drive
See Forest Hills subdvision.

Floyd Street
Charles Lewis Floyd, the superintendent of Montgomery schools from 1889-1914.

Folmar Parkway
Located in Interstate Industrial Park, this street honors Emory Folmar, Montgomery mayor from 1977 to the present.

Forbes Drive (S.)
Capt. A.G. Forbes, the former owner of the property, which was purchased by the federal government for WWI-era Camp Sheridan. See also Vandiver Blvd.

Forest Avenue
See Oak Park.

Forest Brook Lane
Near White's Slough. See Carriage Hills.

Forestdale Drive
One of a series of streets in the Perry Hill subdivision ending with "dale."

Forest Grove Court, Drive
In a series of streets with "tree" and "glen" references.

Forest Hills Drive
See Forest Hills.

■ FOREST HILLS
Developed in the late 1950s to early 1960s by Ray Amos and Billy Moore. Many Forest Hills streets are named after the Robin Hood legend. Botanical references also abound.

Forest Park Drive
In a forested area with other forest references.

Forest Ridge Court
Close to streets with "wood" as part of names: Blythewood, Charingwood, Hollowwood, Saddlewood.

Forsyth Lane
Montgomery's streets frequently reference N. C. cities, and

in this case, a county.

Forte Lane

Adjacent to Young-Forte Park.

Foshee Road

W.S. Foshee, a business and property owner near Maxwell AFB.

Foster Street

Located in an area among several streets named for people. Of note: Stephen Foster wrote many favorite songs sbout the South including "My Old Kentucky Home," "Camptown Races" and "Oh! Susanna." He died at age 37 in 1864 after telling a friend "I'm done for."

Fountain Street

In an area incorporated into city in late 1800s, possibly the former site of a public fountain.

Fournay Street

See King's Hill.

Fowler Street

Honors Confederate Col. William Henry Fowler (1826-67).

Fox Creek Court

Camp Creek flows through this area.

Fox Den Lane

The former site of a fox den on property once owned by Ida Bell Young.

Foxdale Road

See Fox Hollow.

Foxhall Drive

The oldest "fox"-themed street in Montgomery.

■ **FOX HOLLOW**

Developer Bowen Ballard used to enjoy fox hunting and named the streets in Fox Hollow after the sport and its environment.

Fox Hollow Circle, Road

See Fox Hollow.

Foxleigh Court

In a neighborhood of streets with rural references.

Foy Drive

James Foy, a former dean at Auburn University.

Francis Street

Of note: An Autauga native and Creek nation prophet, Josiah Francis, was captured and hanged by Gen. Andrew Jackson in 1818.

Frederick Avenue

Among several streets named for people.

Fredericksburg Drive

C. T. Fitzpatrick named it for the Civil War battle of Fredericksburg (Dec. 1862), in which CSA General Robert E. Lee's forces were victorious.

Freeman Court

In Dalraida amid other last-name references. Possibly for Douglas Southall Freeman, who wrote a Pulitzer-Prize-winning biography of Robert E. Lee.

Freemont Drive †

Of note: John Charles Fremont, a northwest explorer and later senator for Calif., ran for U. S president in 1856 and served as governor of the Arizona Territory (1878-1883).

French Street

Montgomery's key connection to France was the visit of Lafayette in 1825. See "A Hero Rides Our Roads." It is situated among several streets named for people.

Fresno Lane

A Calif. city in an area of grape, date and raisin growing that leads all U.S. counties in the value of agricultural products.

Frontenac Court, Street

Possibly for a 17th-century administrator of New France (American territories).

Frost Street

Among several streets named for people.

Fuller Road, Street

For Mr. Fuller, who was the secretary of the Montgomery Chamber of Commerce for 25 years.

Furnace Street

The location of riverside industry follows the river's bend east from the Old Confederate Powder Magazine to more modern industrial areas.

G

Gabon Way
The name of a Republic of West Africa that is located along the equator.

Gaddy's Court †

Gainesville Street
For a Fla. city.

Gainswood
A plantation near Selma. See Wynlakes.

Galena Avenue
The hometown in Ill. of Robert H. McClellan and Charles Scheerer, real estate speculators of the Cloverdale Land and Development Co. See Cloverdale.

Gantry Court, Drive
In a neighborhood of streets named for people.

Garden Street
Characteristic of Garden Square, where this street is located.

Gardendale Drive (E.)
Near Garden St. and Park Ave.

Garden Homes Circle
Montgomery has several developments of these smaller houses surrounded by enough land for a garden.

Garland Drive
Surname of one of the former town of Cloverdale's original aldermen. See Cloverdale.

Garner Court
In an area of last names for streets.

Garrett Street
A prominent early Montgomery family name.

Gaskell Circle (N. & S.)
James Gaskell, president of First Alabama Bank.

Gas Light Curve
See Carriage Hills.

Gaston Avenue, Court
In a neighborhood of last names used for streets.

Gateway Court, Drive
The entry to the Twin Gates neighborhood.

Garrett Coliseum

In the early 1950's, engineers and architects from all over the world came to Montgomery to study the revolutionary new agricultural center, the State Coliseum. The award-winning plans for the building were submitted by the firm of Sherlock, Smith and Adams, but few people realize that the unique design belonged to a Harvard student working for the firm during the summer. The student was Betty Nicrosi (now Mrs. Vaughn Hill Robison), and the design was her architectural thesis. Plans selected, the coliseum's groundbreaking ceremony was held Aug. 31, 1948.

Gov. James E. "Big Jim" Folsom was in office, and his sister, Ruby Folsom Austin, claims that the idea for the center was based on a Texas agricultural center that she had visited while serving as Alabama's first lady. Upon returning to the state, she said, she "sold James on the idea" and then enlisted the aid of William Walter Garrett, a legislator from Monroe County, to make it a reality. Garrett became totally dedicated to the concept and "badgered the legislature" out of $1.5 million. Construction began in 1949.

The open house and dedication, held Oct. 20-21, 1953, presented two full days of events including cattle judging, horse shows and two concerts by the Lanier High School Band. While this was the formal dedication, the facility had actually been in limited use for two years. The first event to be held there was a country music concert starring Hank Williams, Hank Snow and the Carter Sisters in 1951.

The name of the building was changed in 1963 to honor the man who had worked so hard to ensure that the plan became a reality. "I thought they should have named it after my brother," said Austin.

Gatewood Drive

An entry to Heatherton Heights neighborhood and formerly the site of the White family farm.

Gatsby Court, Drive, Lane

The title character of *The Great Gatsby*, a novel by F. Scott Fitzgerald, the husband of Montgomerian Zelda Sayre Fitzgerald. See Fitzgerald Rd., F. Scott Dr. and Zelda Rd.

Gaylan Court

Possibly a combination of two first or last names.

Gaylord Place †

Geneva Street

A S. Ala. county organized in 1868 and named for Geneva, Switzerland.

Genetta Court

Near Genetta Creek, once known as Bogue Homa (also Houma), an African-American settlement during the late 19th century.

Gentilly Court

Possibly for a local homestead.

George Street

Prev. 9th St. On Maxwell AFB, renamed to honor Lt. Gen. Harold L. George, instructor for the Air Corps Tactical School 1932-36. His assignments culminated with CC of the Air Corps Ferrying Command.

George B. Edmundson Drive

Lawyer and businesman. Another George B. Edmundson was a longtime tax assessor.

George Green Drive (E. & W.)

A Carol Villa street developed by landowner George Green.

George Mull Street

See Highland Gardens.

George Todd Drive

George H. Todd, the founder of a store on Commerce St. specializing in guns and cutlery. The store, established in 1848, is still in business. Although now at a different location, it is one of the city's oldest continuously operating businesses.

Georgena Curve †

Georgetown Drive (N. & S.)

English names were chosen to honor developer David Thames'

English heritage.

Georgia Street
Honors the state of Georgia.

Germany Street
Honors the European country.

Gerrell Court
In a neighborhood using last names for streets.

Ghent Street
The Treaty of Ghent, Belgium, negotiated at the end of the War of 1812, whose naval heroes are commemorated in several major downtown streets.

Gibbs Circle, Court, Drive †

Gibson Court, Street
Mary Clair Gibson Comer, the former owner of an estate on which this street was developed.

Gillespie Drive
A longtime city department head who once owned land where Longmeadow Dr. is now located.

Gilmer Avenue, Court
Francis M. Gilmer, Sr., who was one of the four men involved in a joint venture to rebuild the Exchange Hotel after it was destroyed by fire on Dec. 16, 1818. Or, possibly for Peachy Ridgeway Gilmer, a Va. planter and Montgomery landowner, who was the brother of Gov. Gilmer of Ga.

Girard Street
Possibly related to a settlement that is part of Phenix City in Russell County and named for Stephen Girard, a Philadelphia philanthropist who once owned land in the area.

Glade Court
See Wynlakes.

Glade Park Drive, Loop
See Pecan Grove.

Gladlane Drive
The farm of local developer L.D. Rouse.

Gladstone Drive
Probably for William E. Gladstone, the Labour prime minister of England at various times between 1868 and 1894. The gladstone bag is named for him.

Glen Chase Road

In an British-themed area. The word "glen" means "valley" and is Middle English derived from Scottish-Gaelic. A chase is a privately owned game preserve.

Glenco Court

"Glen" plus the first syllable of this development, Copperfield. A city in Scotland; in a British-themed area.

Glenda Lane

In an area using women's first names for streets.

Glendale Street

Previously Japan Ave., the name was changed during World War II. See also Capitol Heights.

Glenfern Court

See Mosswood.

Glenforest Drive

Depicts a wooded valley.

Glen Grattan

A glen is a valley, and "Grattan" is a Scottish reference.

Glen Iris

Literally translated: spring flowers in a valley.

Glenmore Road

Whiskey distillers.

Glenn Court

In an area of men's and and women's first names used for streets.

Glenn Palmer Avenue

A former orthopedic surgeon at Jackson Hospital, with an office on nearby Pine St., at a time when there were only four orthopedic surgeons in the city. He practiced for over 30 years.

Glenside Court

Developer Jimmy Lowder chose this descriptive name.

Glenwood Road

One of a series of streets in the Perry Hills subdivision ending with "wood." See Farwood Dr., Lakewood Dr.

Gloucester Mews

In an area using the English term for a stable area or side street for the street name. Glouchester is an area in S.W. England.

Gloria Court †

Godfrey Street †

Goldbug Street

A supporter of the gold standard, or a type of beetle. An allusion to a popular story by Edgar Allan Poe.

Golden Gate Drive

The famous bridge in San Francisco.

Golden Rod Court

In a neighborhood with botanical street names. The goldenrod was adopted as the state flower of Ala. in 1927. See Camellia Dr.

Goldthwaite Street

Prominent early Montgomerians: John Goldthwaite, an early settler elected to the first town council; Henry Goldthwaite, an Ala. Supreme Court associate justice (1837-47); and George Goldthwaite, an Ala. Supreme Court associate justice (1851-56) and chief justice (1856), who helped codify Ala. law in 1851 and served as the state's adjutant general during the Civil War. He died in 1879 and is buried in Oakwood Cemetery.

Goode Street

Samuel Goode, an active local developer with George Clayton in late 1800s. See Clayton St.

Goodwyn Court, Drive

John L. Goodwyn, a former Montgomery mayor (1947-51), who was often referred to by the nickname "Wank."

Gordon Court, Street

St.: CSA Gen. John B. Gordon, commander of the 6th Alabama Regiment of the Army of Northern Virginia. He was wounded five times at Antietam in defense of the sunken road, lived to return to battle and later wrote *Reminiscences of the Civil War*. Ct.: See Regency Park.

Gorgas Street

Gen. Josiah Gorgas, Confederate hero, and his son, Dr. William C. Gorgas, major general and surgeon general of the U.S. Army, who eliminated yellow fever in Cuba and Panama, allowing for construction of the Panama Canal.

Governors Drive

Developed during the administratrion of Governor George

C. Wallace. Across South Blvd. from Wallace Dr.

Grace Street †

Grady Street

Possibly for the town by the same name in S. Montgomery County.

Graham Street

Prev. 1st St. The Graham family owned the surrounding land known as "Graham's Wood" or "The Pines" and later part of the Cloverdale development. William Graham, an early member of the family, owned a store on Dexter Ave. (when it was still Market St.) and was Montgomery's first mayor. See Cloverdale.

Grand Oak Court

See Halcyon South.

Graves Street

Gov. Bibb Graves (1927-31) or David Bibb Graves, a member of the House of Representatives and the state's adjutant general (1907-11), who organized the lst Ala. Cavalry Regiment during WWI and, later, the Ala. department of the American Legion.

Greecham Drive †

Green Acres Court, Road

The Green Acres neighborhood was developed on former farmland.

Greenbriar Road

A resort located in the Blue Ridge Mountains.

Greenbrook Drive

In a neighborhood with outdoor themes used for street names.

Greenchase Circle, Drive

Adjacent to Arrowhead Country Club Golf course.

Green Forest Court, Drive

Descriptive, generic.

Greenleaf Drive

Entryway to Southlawn.

Green Oaks Drive

In Forest Park.

Green Park Drive

Street in Wildwood named by Bill Jennings.

Green Pine Lane

So named for the multitude of trees in the area. See Forest Hills.

Greenpine Circle, Drive

Near a park in Westview Gardens.

Green Ridge Court, Road

So named for the multitude of trees in the area. See Forest Hills.

Greensboro Court, Drive

Ala. river city. Also N.C. city.

Greenview Drive

A street located near the Standard Country Club and golf course.

Greenville Street

S. central Ala. town named for a S.C. city.

Green Way, Green Way Place

Near Woodmere Park.

Greenwood Street

Borders the cemetery of the same name.

Greg Drive

See Forest Hills.

Gregory Avenue †

Grenada Drive

An island in the eastern Caribbean located 150 miles southwest of Barbados.

Greta Place

Retired Col. Hugh Hughes, a West Point graduate employed by Ballard Realty for 20 years, gave several streets in the Woodmere subdivision feminine German names. See Astrid Pl., Heidi Pl. and Helga Pl.

Greyfield Drive

See Wynlakes.

Greyhound Drive (N. & S.)

A popular swift English dog. The whippet is a smaller version.

Greystone Drive, Place

A generic stone commonly used in British construction. Also, the name of the bank building on Commerce St., one of the city's early "skyscrapers."

Groom Street †

Grove Street
A part of the Wilson Grove property in 1883.

Grove Hill
Located near Forest Park and Green Oaks Dr.

Groveland Drive
See Pecan Grove Estates.

Grove Park Drive
A route that goes to Gunter Grove and cuts through former pecan groves.

Grovewood Court, Drive
Formerly a pecan orchard belonging to Clyde Jennings.

Guilford Road
One of a group of N.C. areas used for street names. The Revolutionary War Battle of Guilford Courthouse was fought there. Also, the birthplace of Dolley Madison.

Gundy Street
Situated in an industrial area of N. Montgomery where the streets are named for people.

Gunn Road
The Gunn family once owned this property south of the Atlanta Hwy.

Gunster Road †

Gunter Park Drive (E. & W.)
The Gunter Industrial Park is named for and located adjacent to Gunter Annex.

Gunter Street
Charles G. Gunter, an early settler who was a planter, lawyer and state legislator. Reputed to be one of the wealthiest gentlemen in the county, Gunter was a strong supporter of the Confederacy and father of Col. W.A. Gunter, Harris Gunter and Mrs. Frank Elmore. When the South lost the war, he moved to Brazil.

Guymar Road
Builders Carl Guy and I.D. Martin.

Gwynnbrook Road
Near Baldwin Brook.

Gunter Annex
of Maxwell AFB

In July 1940 the city leased its only airport to the War Department. Two months later, the Army Air Corps Basic Flying School was activated on the site. War Department Order No. 2, dated Feb. 10, 1941, designated the newly federalized facility as "Gunter Field" honoring the late Mayor William Adams Gunter, who died on Dec. 4, 1940, after serving 27 years as head of Montgomery's city government. Mayor Gunter had participated in the development of Maxwell Field, established a municipal airport despite opposition and was instrumental in securing land leases that ensured that the military flying school was established in Montgomery rather than at the alternate sites of Selma, Troy or Albany, Ga. In its 55-year history, the military facility has been designated a field, a base and a station. It is now an annex of Maxwell AFB.

H

Haardt Drive (N. & S.)
John H. Haardt, a local real estate developer.

Habersham Road
See "Montgomery's Own Philadelphia Story."

Hackberry Lane
In an area of tree names for streets.

Hackel Drive †

Haddington Road
In an area of family names used for streets.

Hadley Street †

Hagan Road †

■ HALCYON
Developers and investors named several streets for cities, town-

ships and streets in the United Kingdom. Halcyon South's developers used landscape features for street names. Halcyon, the name of a country home on Halcyon Hill situated adjacent to Auburn University at Montgomery in E. Montgomery, means "peaceful and quiet."

Halcyon Boulevard, Drive
See Halcyon.

Halcyon Downs Loop
See Halcyon.

Halcyon Forest Trail
See Halcyon.

Halcyon Summit Drive
See Halcyon.

Hale Street
For the Ala. county organized in 1867 and named for Col. Stephen F. Hale. Of interest: James Hale, a former slave of Dr. William O. Baldwin, who later became one of the wealthiest African-Americans working as a contractor. He built Hale's Infirmary to memorialize his two children. His daughter married Dr. Cornelius Dorsett, Montgomery's first African-American physician.

Haley Court †

Halifax Court, Lane
Near other streets named for British cities. Halifax is a borough northeast of Manchester, an industrial center.

Hall Street
Bolling Hall, native Georgian, moved to Montgomery in 1817 and established the Chestnut Wood Estate, which later became Oak Park; served as a congressman for Ala. and addressed Gen. Lafayette during his visit to Montgomery in 1825. See Oak Park, LaFayette St.

Halston Court
See McGehee Pl.

Hambleton Road
See Taylor Crossing.

Hamilton Circle, Street
Possibly for Albert James Hamilton (1838-1901), member of Alabama legislature from 1869-1872 and 1874-1875. He donated the land for Hamilton, Ala.

Hamner Street

Bishop Nicholas Hamner Cobbs (1796-1861), an opponent of secession who became the first bishop of the Diocese of Ala., Protestant Episcopal Church, in 1844.

Hampton Street

The Civil War ironclads *Monitor* and *Merrimac* fought at Hampton Rds., Va.

Handel Court, Drive

Possibly Baroque music master George Fredrick Handel, composer of *Messiah*.

Hanley Street

Prev. 13th St. on Maxwell AFB, renamed to honor Maj. Gen. Thomas J. Hanley, a 1921 graduate and subsequently an instructor of the Air Corps Tactical School. He served as Commanding General of the Eastern Flying Command 1943; CG of AAF in Burma-India 1945; and CG of the 11th AF 1946.

Hanloe Court †

Hannon Street

Part of the Hannon and Jones subdivision in late 1800s.

Hanover Drive

The House of Hanover, a line of British monarchs including George I, George II, George III, George IV, William IV and Victoria, 1714-1901.

Hanrick Street

Edward "Horseshoe Heel" (also "Horseshoe Ned") Hanrick, a wealthy early land speculator from Ireland. He donated the northeast corner of Lawrence and Adams streets to his church in 1831. In 1834 St. Peter's opened on that corner.

Hansell Street

Prev. 5th St., on Maxwell AFB, renamed to honor Maj. Gen. Haywood S. Hansell, one of the "Men on the Flying Trapeze." He served as a member of the Air War Plans division in 1941; CG of the 1st and 3rd Bomber Wings in 1942-43; Chief of Staff of the 20th AF; and CG of the 21st Bomber Command.

Happiness Avenue

Offered by the developer as a joyful place to live.

Happy Hollow Drive

Located at the bottom of a hill.

Harbinger Court
A portent or symbol of the future. See Wyndridge.

Hardaway Street
James H. Hardaway, a local property owner in the late 1800s.

Harding Close
A member of the Hill family, who once owned the land.

Hardwick Street
William Henry Hardwick, a clothing buyer and a former editorial writer for the *Montgomery Advertiser*.

Harmon Street
See Highland Gardens.

Harmony Street
A theme of musical or family cooperation.

Harness Hill Drive
Before development, the area had a ranch atmosphere, says area resident June Collier. Refers to horses' harnesses.

Harold Street
See Highland Gardens.

Harriet Street †

Harris Street
See Highland Gardens.

Harrison Road
Possibly for Benjamin Harrison, the 23rd U. S. president. He died March 13, 1901 at age 67. Teddy Roosevelt once called him a "cold-blooded...old psalm-singing Indianapolis politician."

Harrogate Hill
See Wynlakes.

Hartford Street
A city in Conn.

Harvard Road
The University in Cambridge, Mass., founded in 1636. See College Grove.

Harvest Hill Court
See Sturbridge.

Harvest Ridge Drive
See Sturbridge.

Harvest Way
See Young Place.

Hastings Court
A Carol Villa street that was probably named by newer developers than the Johnson family, original owners.

Hatcher Court †

Hatfield Road
An area property-owning family.

Hathaway Place
Anne Hathaway, who married William Shakespeare in 1582. In an English-themed area.

Hatton Avenue †

Havelock Lane
Of interest: Sir Henry Havelock invented a cap that used a flap of cloth to protect the back of the neck.

Haven Drive, Lane (W.)
Dr.: Site of East Haven Assisted Living. La.: In an area of last names used for streets.

Hawthorn Drive
A small thorny tree. Near Boxwood and similar references.

Hawthorne Street
Located on Maxwell AFB.

Haynes Lane
The family who owned Haynes Turkey Farm also owned land in this area off Perry Hill Rd.

Hayneville Road
The primary route to the city of Hayneville.

Hazel Hedge Lane
Developed on the estate formerly owned by Mrs. Nash Reid, who selected the name.

Healey Street †

Hearn Street
For the Methodist Episcopal circuit-riding minister Ebenezer Hearn (1794-1862), who died in Montgomery.

Heath Drive
An evergreen shrub or small tree usually adorned with rose or purple flowers.

Heatherbrooke Court

Suggests rural attributes of this land that was formerly owned by the Hill family.

■ HEATHERTON HEIGHTS

A native of Pittsburgh, Don Cameron selected names for this area from a Pittsburgh phone directory.

Heatherton Drive

In Heatherton Heights.

Heathrow Downs, Drive, Place

A major London airport. See Wynlakes.

Heidi Place

Retired Col. Hugh Hughes, a West Point graduate employed by Ballard Realty, gave several streets in Woodmere feminine German names. See Astrid Pl., Greta Pl. and Helga Pl.

Heilpern Street

Eugene Heilpern, the owner of Heilpern's General Merchandise Store. He also owned property in this area and helped to develop it. The Heilpern family came to Montgomery at the turn of the century.

Helga Place

Retired Col. Hugh Hughes, a West Point graduate employed by Ballard Realty, gave several streets in Woodmere feminine German names. See Astrid Pl., Greta Pl. and Heidi Pl.

Hemon Road

A combination of Henrietta and Monty, wife and son of Lowder developer Jerry Wills. See Whitney Dr.

Henle Street

Sam Henle, an employee of Heilpern's General Merchandise Store, owned by Eugene Heilpern, a local property owner and real estate developer. The Heilpern family came from Germany at the turn of the century.

Henry Drive

A series of English monarchs. Also, an Ala. County organized in 1819 and named for Patrick Henry of Va.

Herbert Drive

Possibly for Col. Hilary A. Herbert, President Grover Cleveland's secretary of the navy. He died in 1919 and is buried in Oakwood Cemetery.

Hercules Street

Part of the Hugh Simpson subdivision in 1907. Parallel to Ajax; both are Greek mythological heroes.

Heritage Oak Court

See Halcyon South.

Hermitage Drive

Andrew Jackson's home located in Nashville, Tenn.

Herron Street

An early Montgomery family who married Thoringtons. Sarah Parker Herron (1826-99) worked at the Ladies' Hospital during the Civil War. She died in 1899 and is buried at Oakwood Cemetery.

Heth Street

Possibly for the eighth letter of the Hebrew alphabet.

Heustess Street

Jimmy Heustess, a promoter of Capitol Heights.

Hibiscus Street

A plant with showy, brightly colored flowers. See Pecan Grove Estates.

Hickman Street †

Hickory Drive (E.), Street

A North American tree noted for its particularly hard wood. Dr.: See Maxwell AFB. St.: Near Wares Ferry Rd.

Hickory Hill Court

In a neighborhood using tree names for streets.

Hidden Meadow Drive

In a neighborhood of outdoor references.

High Street

The highest point relative to the city (now the downtown area), based on a tradition in English and Scottish towns that had a High St.

Highfield Drive

In an area formerly used for cultivation by the Hill family.

Highland Avenue

A development of the Highland Park Improvement Co. begun in 1887. It is an extension of High St. where traffic changes from two to four lanes.

Highland Court (S.)

The elevation of the land increases as one travels north into the city past this street.

■ HIGHLAND GARDENS

This neighborhood, developed after WWI, has many streets bearing female first names and surnames probably of some significance to the developer.

■ HIGHLAND PARK

A residential development begun in the 1880s by the Highland Park Development Co., this area was the first true streetcar suburb in Montgomery. The streets' names were designated as numbers, botanical references and family names of the developers. The area is now known as Oak Park.

Highland Village Road

The location of the Highland Village Youth Center.

High Point Road

One of several streets named after cities in N.C.

High Ridge Court

Named by developer C.T. Fitzpatrick.

Hilda Drive †

Hill Street

On Hill family property. See Hillwood.

Hillabee Court, Drive

Hilibi, an ancient Upper Creek town situated near a creek; derived from Creek "hilapki" or "hilikbi" (quick).

Hillcrest Lane

Named for the lay of the land. See Forest Hills Subdivision.

Hilldale Drive

For its slightly rolling terrain.

Hill Hedge Drive

Named by Boyd and Hardie McGehee, the former owners of the land.

Hilliard Street

Henry W. Hilliard, a Civil War-era Methodist minister and prominent attorney. He died in 1892 and is buried at Oakwood Cemetery.

Hillman Court, Street

The Hillmans, whose home is now a Catholic nursing home.

Hillmar Lane
Possibly a combination of two names.

Hillsboro Road
A Carol Villa street named for the lay of the land.

Hillside Oaks, Road
In a neighborhood with tree names used for streets.

Hilltop
Located near Hillside Oaks.

Hillview Close
Located on land formerly owned by the Hill family.

Hillwood Drive
On former lands of Luther Leonidas Hill, Methodist minister and founder in Montgomery of the prominent Hill family.

Hinchcliff Road
A British-sounding name in an area using an English motif for street names.

Hitching Post Court, Lane
See Carriage Hills.

Hi View Lane
A Perry Hills street named for its view.

Hiwassee Drive
The Cherokee word for "savannah."

Hobbie Drive
Richard Hobbie, a Montgomery developer and contractor.

Hodges Avenue
Prev. Avenue C, on Gunter Annex of Maxwell AFB, renamed to honor 2nd Lt. Patrick W. Hodges, the third American to die in an aircraft accident while stationed at Gunter Field.

Holbrook Drive †

Holcombe Street
Hosea Holcombe (1780-1841), who preached across the state and presided over the State Baptist Convention, which he helped found.

Holland Drive
The Netherlands; see Forest Hills.

Holliday Drive
Possibly for Judy Holliday, a film actress who was popular at

the time of this development.

Hollis Drive
See Halcyon.

Holloway Park †

Hollow Wood Drive
Among a group of streets with "wood" as part of names: Charing Wood, Saddlewood, Blythewood; near Forest Ridge. (Appears on some maps and street signs as one word.)

Holly Street
See Highland Park.

Holly Brook Drive
See Fox Hollow.

Hollylock Court
See Mosswood.

Holly Ridge Drive
Holly bushes abound on this woodsy Bellehurst street. See "Montgomery's Own Philadelphia Story."

Holt Street
E.R. and Mary Holt, developers in 1890s. Of note: Lucy Holt, wife of the Rev. Dr. William Holt, a soldier in the Revolution, died in 1847 and is buried in Oakwood cemetery.

Home Place
A welcoming name in any subdivision.

Homeview Street
Probably named before city annexation in 1910.

Honey Bee Court
See Regency Park.

Honeysuckle Court, Road
A clinging vine with fragrant flowers that is very common to the area.

Hope Road
Probably for Hope, England, located south of Liverpool.

Hopper Street
Joseph D. Hopper, one of those who acquired the land for the Capitol Heights area in 1856 and helped to develop it.

Horace Street
The Roman lyric poet of great influence on English literature.

Horseshoe Circle

In an area with several references to horses.

Houser Street

See Chisholm.

Houston Place, Street

Pl: Sam Houston, a hero of the Texas Revolution. St.: Located in an area of the city that was in the originial 1819 incorporation. An Ala. county organized in 1903 and named for Gov. George S. Houston (1874-78).

Howard Street

Near Maxwell AFB: Possibly for 2nd Lt. James A. Howard, who was killed in an airplane crash at Maxwell Field in 1939. Another street is located in the Garden District parallel to Frederick Ave., in a neighborhood with streets named for people.

Howe Street †

Hubbard Street

Dr. Brannon Hubbard and his wife, Caroline, bought this part of the old Fairview Plantation lands in the 1920s. See Fairview Ave.

Hudson Court

See "Montgomery's Own Philadelphia Story."

Hugh Street †

Hull Street (N. & S.)

War of 1812 Naval Commodore Isaac Hull, who commanded *The Constitution* to the first American victory on Aug. 12, 1812, when he defeated the British *Guerriere*.

Hunt Street

The early Ala. pioneer John Hunt, for whom the N. Ala. city of Huntsville was named.

Hunter Lane, Street

La: One of three parallel streets named for people. St.: Located near Hunter Station Park.

Hunter Loop Road

A Hunter family once owned the store located at the intersection of Washington Ferry Rd. and Hunter Loop.

Hunters Branch Drive

Situated in Cross Creek, between Whites and Baldwin sloughs.

Hunting Creek Road
Located between Whites and Baldwin sloughs.

Huntingdon Court
Jim Wilson, the developer of Wynlakes, is a supporter of Huntingdon College. The 58-acre campus was named for Selina, Countess of Huntingdon, who was noted for her influence in the Wesleyan movement. See Wynlakes.

Huntington Street †

Huntly Drive
Situated among several streets that are named for people.

Hurlston Drive
See Regency Park.

Hutchinson Street
J. Hutchinson, an attorney and merchant who moved to the area in the 1820s. In 1860, J. D. Hutchinson helped organize the Alabama Insurance Co.

Hyde Park Drive
The famous park in London, England.

I

I-85 Parkway
Intended as an access street for I-85.

Idlewild Court
Originally the name of the JFK airport in New York, which was renamed in 1963.

Industrial Drive
Located in Capitol Industrial Plaza.

Ingle Court, Drive
See Chisholm.

Inner Circle
An area on Maxwell AFB where the senior officers' quarters are located.

Inn South Avenue
The location of the Inn South Motel.

Interstate Court, Park Drive
Both streets run through executive areas off I-85.

Intervale Road
Low land, especially along a river; in an area of where many streets have "brook" in the names.

Inverness Road
A town in northern Scotland; in an area of British-themed streets.

Inwood Drive
In the woods near Alpine Dr.

Ira Lane
Realtor Ira Betts, the owner of Betts Realty and Appraisal Service. In a neighborhood of streets with first names.

Iris Court, Lane
A colorful spring flower in a neighborhood of streets named for flowering plants.

Ironwood Drive
In a neighborhood with botanical street names, especially trees.

Iroquois Court
Known as the Six Nations, comprised of the Cayuga, Mohawk, Oneida, Onondago, Seneca, and Tuscarora tribes.

Ivy Lane, Street
Any of several clinging vines common to the E. United States.

Ivy Green Drive
See Wynlakes.

J

Jackson Street (N. & S.)
Andrew Jackson (1767-1845), who through his victory at Horseshoe Bend in the War of 1812 and the subsequent Treaty of Fort Jackson made settlement in Montgomery possible. In 1817, when Montgomery was established, Jackson St. was on the perimeter.

Jackson Ferry Road
Old ferry crossing on the Alabama River. Many of the streets in this neighborhood are surnames, which were probably for prominent people related to the development of this area or important to the ferry that once existed in the area. One such individual was Gen. Crawford M. Jackson, a veteran of nu-

merous Civil War campaigns. Before the war, he served as the Autauga Co. representative to the state legislature. He is buried in Oakwood Cemetery.

Jacobs Court
See Young Place.

James Avenue, Court, Road
Ave: Probably for James Steptoe Pinckard, the president of the Capitol Heights Development Co. Ct., Rd.: Possibly for the 1960s mayor Earl James.

Jamestown Court, Drive
The first permanent English settlement in the New World (1607), in Va.

Jameswood Court
See "Montgomery's Own Philadelphia Story."

Jan Drive
In a neighborhood of streets with first names, many of them women's.

Japonica Street
A flowering shrub, also called Japanese quince, in a neighborhood of streets using the names of flowers.

Jasmine Road
A Southern shrub with fragrant white or yellow flowers.

Jason Court
Probably a family name important to the development of Garden Square.

Jay Street
Connects Marlborough St. to Salem Dr., "as the crow flies."

Jean Street
In a neighborhood of streets with first names.

Jeff Davis Avenue (E. & W.)
Jefferson Davis, the only president of the Confederate States of America, inaugurated in Montgomery in 1861. He died Dec. 6, 1889, and was buried in his Confederate uniform in Richmond, Va.

Jefferson Street
Thomas Jefferson (1743-1826), the third president of the U.S.

Jeffrey Drive
In a neighborhood of streets with first names.

Jenella Drive

The wife of developer Charles York.

Jenkins Lane

Property owners in the area.

Jennifer Lane

See Regency Park.

Jesse Court

The foreman on the farm of W. Inge Hill, Sr., for over 40 years.

John Brown Avenue

A property owner who donated much of the surrounding land to Alabama State University.

John Dunn Court (E. & W.)

The son of investor Johnny Dunn.

John Morris Avenue †

John Overton Drive

A bondsman for major contracting firms.

Johnson Avenue

Probably an important figure in the development of the Boylston Mills area. See Boylston.

Johnson Street

Three different streets in Montgomery. One is in Cottage Hill. Another is named for T. M. Johnson, one of the owners of the area known as the Johnson plat, or W. A. Johnson, owner of property on which the Highland Gardens subdivision was developed. See Highland Gardens. The third street is in Chisholm and possibly honors Andrew Johnson, the 17th U.S. president who took office when Lincoln was assassinated. He died July 31, 1875, and was buried in compliance with his statement: "When I die, I desire no better winding sheet than the Stars and Stripes, and no softer pillow than the Constitution."

Johnstown Court, Drive

A town in Penn. remembered for a devastating flood on May 31, 1889. See also "Montgomery's Own Philadelphia Story."

Jones Street

Part of Hannon and Jones subdivision in late 1800s. Also of note: Thomas Goode Jones was the state's governor (1890-94) during the same period and may share the honors here.

He is buried in Oakwood Cemetery.

Jordan Street
Possibly related to the Elmore County settlement named for John L. Jordan, the area's first postmaster.

Joryne Drive †

Joseph Street
Joseph M. Kennedy, a local brick manufacturer as well as a wood, paint, blind and sash dealer. Kennedy St. was also named for him.

Jule Drive
In a neighborhood of family names.

Julia Street
Probably a name in the Ryan family, owners of the property in 1871.

Juliette Street
Adjacent to Persons Alley, developed in 1920s. A name in the Persons family, with the sixth-generation Juliette born in 1994.

June Street
In a neighborhood using family names for streets.

Juniper Street (N. & S.)
See Maxwell AFB. Also, one of the three telephone exchanges that existed in the city prior to 1941.

Juniper Tree Lane
In a neighborhood with botanical street names, especially trees.

K

Kahn Street
Harry Kahn, who was an area landowner during the early days of the city. Harry was one of 11 children of Maurice Kahn, who left his native Alsace-Lorraine (France), made a fortune in diamonds in Brazil, bought and sold sugar enterprises in La. and Miss., and who, traveling through Montgomery in 1871, noticed that it was ideally positioned between New Orleans and Atlanta for a wholesale grocery business to supply country stores. This business became Schloss and Kahn.

Kansas Street
The state of Kansas.

Karen Road

See "Montgomery's Own Philadelphia Story."

Kathmoor Drive

See Halycon.

Katrina Place

Retired Col. Hugh Hughes, a West Point graduate employed by Ballard Realty, gave several streets in Woodmere feminine German names. See Greta Pl., Heida Pl., and Helga Pl.

Keating Drive

See Chisholm.

Keifer Drive †

Also appears on some maps and lists as "Kiefer."

Kelly Lane, Street

A prominent landowning Montgomery family. La.: in Cloverland. St.: in Western Hills. Also a street on Maxwell AFB that memorializes Lt. G.E.M. Kelly, the first fatality in flight training. He was the first Army pilot and second officer to lose his life in military aviation. While training at Ft. Sam Houston, Texas, the Curtis biplane that he was flying lost a brace from one of the wheels. Lt. Kelly crashed the aircraft into the ground to avoid hitting the camp of the 11th Infantry on May 10, 1911.

Kelly Anne Court

A Fox Hollow street, possibly named by neighborhood developer Bowen Ballard.

Kempton Drive †

Kenilworth Street

Located off the Birmingham Highway; a city in England located southeast of Birmingham. Kenilworth is the county seat of the Earl of Leicester, a favorite of Queen Elizabeth (1558-1603). One of five parallel streets bearing family or given names with British connotations.

Kennedy Street

Joseph M. Kennedy, a brick manufacturer as well as a wood, paint, blind and sash dealer. See Joseph St.

Kenny Avenue

In a neighborhood using family names for streets.

Kensington Street

The name of the suburban area owned by W.C. Holt in 1891.

Kent Street

A county in southeast England; a royal dukedom in Great Britain; a brand of smoking tobacco (in a series of streets named for cigarettes—Marlborough St. and Salem Dr).

Kentucky Oaks

In a neighborhood of streets with names derived from horse racing.

Kenwood Street †

Kenyon Road

A Carol Villa street that was probably named by developers other than the Johnson family, who originally owned the land.

Kerri Circle †

Kershaw Street

Located in an industrial neighborhood, the street honors the Kershaw family, founders of Kershaw Manufacturing Co., Inc.

Kevin Court

In a neighborhood of streets using people's first names.

Key Street

Francis Scott Key (1779-1843), the author of the lyrics of "The Star-Spangled Banner," written during the War of 1812.

Keystone Street

A central stone in an arch.

Kim Lane

In a neighborhood using first names for streets.

Kimball Street

Kimball Manufacturing, producers of Victorian reproductions.

Kimberly Street †

King's Hill

Some of the street names in this subdivision are surnames which were probably for people important in the development of this area.

King Street

Prev. N. Capitol St., it now honors William Rufus King of Selma, the only Alabamian to serve as vice president of the U.S., elected in 1853. He took the oath of office in Matanzas, Cuba, returned to Selma, and died the same year he took office.

Kingsbury Drive
The middle name of developer William Thames, Sr.

Kings Cliff Road
Situated in a neighborhood with an outdoor theme.

Kingswood Road
In English Village. An urban district in southwest England, primarily residential suburb of Bristol.

Kippax Street †

Kirksey Avenue †

Kirkpatrick Avenue E.
Prev. Avenue C, on Maxwell AFB, the street memorializes Lt. Everett Kirkpatrick, the second person to be killed in an airplane accident at Maxwell Field. He died on March 1, 1921.

Kirkwood Drive
See Halcyon.

Kiwanis Street
A civic organization, founded in 1915, which fosters human and spiritual values.

Knightsbridge Curve
A city in England; in a English-themed neighborhood.

Knollgate Road
A small, rounded hill; parallel to Matterhorn St.

Knollwood Drive
Suggestive of a small, rounded hill in the trees.

Knox Street
William Knox (1800-64), the founder of the Central Bank of Alabama, builder of what became the First White House of the Confederacy, and father of Robert Henderson Knox, a former state legislator.

Kobe Court
A city in Japan, port and manufacturing center.

Kroy Drive
York Developers, spelled backwards.

Kruse Street †

Kuter Street
Prev. 6th St., on Maxwell AFB, renamed to honor Gen. Lawrence S. Kuter. He served as CG of the 1st Bomber Wing in 1942, of the Allied Tactical Air Forces in 1943, and other

assignments before becoming Air University commander in 1953.

Kyser Court

The Kyser family owned and developed the land. Some family members hoped for "boulevard," but had to settle for "court."

L

Laconia Street

An ancient city of southern Greece, part of Sparta.

Lafayette Street

The Marquis de Lafayette (1757-1834), a French hero of the American Revolution who visited Montgomery in 1825. See "A Hero Rides Our Roads."

Lagoon Park Drive

A natural feature of Lagoon Park and the municipal golf course.

Lake Street

A lake was originally planned near this site in the Highland and Oak Park developments.

Lake Bridge Road

Located in Vaughn Lakes development, which includes two ponds developed from Whites Slough.

Lake Forest Court, Drive

See Arrowhead West.

Lakeland Lane

In an area near a developed lake.

Lakeridge Drive, Loop

Dr.: See Wynlakes; Loop: near a developed lake area.

Lakeshire Street

See Carriage Hills.

Lakeside Court

See Arrowhead West.

Lakeview Drive

Developed and named by Don Cameron. A native of Pittsburgh, he chose names from the Pittsburgh phone directory.

A Hero Rides Our Roads

Fifty naked Creek warriors led by Chilly McIntosh, the son of the Indian general William McIntosh, greeted Gen. Gilbert du Motier, the Marquis de Lafayette, on the eastern bank of the Chattahoochee River. On the western bank stood the delegation sent by Gov. Israel Pickens to welcome the former commander of the Continental Army of Virginia to Alabama. The elegantly attired officials and the unclothed native Americans joined to form the escort for the aristocratic visitor as he and his lavishly equipped party began their journey over Alabama's roads and down Montgomery's streets.

The entourage—including the general's only son, George Washington Lafayette—proceeded down the Federal Road, and on the afternoon of April 2, 1825, they arrived at a tavern near Mt. Meigs owned by Walter B. Lucas. The tavern was "done up" in honor of Lafayette, and a crowd had gathered for a glimpse of the celebrated visitor.

On Sunday morning, April 3, the ever-increasing group took to the road again to convey one of the nation's most beloved heroes to Montgomery. He was met atop Goat Hill by Gov. Pickens and "nearly every soul" in the town, as well as hundreds from surrounding rural areas.

After the city's band finished a rendition of "Hail to the Chief," dignitaries offered eloquent speeches lapped up by the crowd along with gallons of the finest locally distilled spirits. The 67-year-old soldier and his party then marched down Market Street to Court Square and Commerce Street to the home of John Edmondson, where he spent the night.

Robert J. Ware, John Caffy and other veterans met Lafayette the following day to share reminiscences of the Revolutionary War. The meeting was extremely emotional but in no way dampened the excitement of the festivities that followed.

A fund of $17,000 had been established by the state legislature and augmented by contributions from the town's generous citizens to ensure that the general had the best of everything the state had to offer. At a grand ball at Feeny's Tavern, on the corner of Commerce and Tallapoosa streets, many of the local ladies danced with the illustrious general until shortly before midnight. Lafayette rested at the home of John Ginrat in preparation for the remainder of his excursion.

For weeks following his departure, the residents of the town related every word spoken by the only surviving general of the American Revolution. The local paper, *The Montgomery Republican*, reported every event. Years later, the visit was still being proclaimed as the "greatest single day" in the history of the city. On July 8, 1858, one correspondent wrote: "Such a calvacade [sic] never traveled that [Federal] road before or since." The same can still be said of the city's streets.

Lakewood Drive
One of a series of streets in the Perry Hills subdivision ending with "wood," such as Farwood Dr., Glenwood Rd.

Lamar Road
Harold Lamar, an area landowner. Of interest: Lamar County was organized in 1867 and named for Sen. L. Q. C. Lamar, of Miss.

Lamco Drive
Lowder, Aronov and Moore, partners in development of the warehouse area on this street as well as the nearby shopping center.

Lamuck Street †

Lancaster Circle, Lane
John Lancaster Goodwyn, justice of the Ala. Supreme Court who married into the Hill family, prominent local landowners.

Land Circle †

Landmark Court, Drive, Place
In Landmark Estates. One source said the developer named

this area for Landmarks Foundation, concerned with historic preservation of Montgomery, while another said that it merely means "a feature distinguishing the neighborhood."

Landsdowne Drive

A famous house in Natchez, Miss.

Lanier Court

Near Lanier High School and named after Sidney Lanier, the poet. Lanier was captured by Union forces at Chancellorsville and imprisoned. After the war, he moved to Montgomery and worked at the Exchange Hotel while writing *Tiger-Lilies*, a war novel. Later, he taught at Prattville Academy.

Larchmont Drive

City in New York.

Laredo Court

Twin cities in Mexico and U.S. In an area of streets in Gunter Grove named for cities.

Largo Lane

Named for the largest of the Florida keys, it is located appropriately in Sunshine Acres.

La Rhoda Street

In an area of Highland Gardens using women's names for streets.

Lark Drive

A bird that is noted for its sustained, melodious song.

Larkin Court, Lane

The Larkin family owned land in the Bellehurst subdivision, where these streets are located.

Larkspur Court

In a neighborhood with botanical street names.

Larkwood Drive

Backs up to a wooded area.

La Salle Street

Probably named for Robert Cavelier, Sieur de la Salle, a French explorer who settled in Canada in 1666 and later navigated the Ohio and Mississippi rivers to the sea. He named the area Louisiana. He was murdered near the Brazos River in Texas.

Latimer Street

In an area of last names used for streets.

Lauderdale Street

Ft. Lauderdale, Fla., or for the Ala. county organized in 1818 and named for Col. James Lauderdale of Tenn.

Lauramac Court

See Regency Park.

Laurel Lane

In an area of botanical names; laurel is an evergreen shrub or small tree of the genus *laurus*.

Laurelwood Lane

See Laurel La.

Lavender Drive

Old world plants having clusters of small purplish flowers. An oil used in perfumes is extracted from these plants.

La Verne Lane

In a neighborhood of first names used for streets.

Lawndale Lane

See Pecan Grove Estates.

Lawnwood Court, Drive (E. & W.)

In Woodcrest Park, themed with "wood" in names.

Lawrence Street (N. & S.)

War of 1812 Naval Commodore James Lawrence (1781-1813), who commanded the *Chesapeake*, lost to the British ship the *Sherman*, at the battle at Lake Erie. He is also famous for his dying words: "Don't give up the ship."

Layton Road

A Carol Villa street probably named by developers after the sale of the land by the Johnson family.

Lazy Brook Lane

See Carriage Hills.

LeBron Avenue, Court, Road

Prev. Earl Ave. A.W. LeBron, a treasurer and major stockholder of Cloverdale Homes Development Co. in 1908, who was originally from Galena, Ill. One of the first aldermen of Cloverdale.

Ledyard Drive, Place

Robert E. Ledyard, a former landowner in this area.

Lee Street

Robert E. Lee, the Confederate general for whom Lee High School is also named, as well as Lee County.

LeGrand Place

Kate E. LeGrand, owner of the development around the park of the same name. Descendant of a family which was part of the original Olive and Vine colony.

Lehigh Street

Both a river and a college in Penn.

Leicester Drive

In an English-themed area. Leicestershire in England is a manufacturing region.

LeMay Plaza

Prev. 2nd St., on Maxwell AFB, renamed to honor Gen. Curtis E. LeMay. LeMay holds the distinction of serving the longest tenure of major command in the history of the U.S. Air Force by serving as Commander of the Strategic Air Command from 1948 to 1957. He was the USAF Chief of Staff in 1961. LeMay was also the former Gov. George Wallace's vice presidential running mate.

Lemon Street

A citrus tree. Parallel to railroad bisecting Day St.

Lenny Lane

In an area of first names used for streets.

Lenora Street

Local brick manufacturer Joseph M. Kennedy's daughter; see Joseph and Kennedy streets.

Lenox Court

In an area of English-themed names. Possibly named for Lenox Square in Atlanta.

Leola Street

Cities in Penn. and S.D.

Leonard Road

In an area of first and last names used for streets.

Leonidas Drive

Honors local landowner Luther Leonidas Hill.

Le Ruth Avenue †

Lester Lane †

Levenson Road †

Lewis Street (N. & S.)

Possibly for David P. Lewis, Alabama's governor from 1872-1874.

Lewis Lane

Reputedly named for Lewes, England. Of note: Dixon H. Lewis ran unsuccessfully for U. S. Senate against William Rufus King during the state's first legislative session and again in 1850.

Lexington Road

Cities in Ky. and N.C. and site of a Revolutionary War battle in Mass.

L. H. Hamilton

Minister of Mt. Sinai Baptist Church.

Libby Street

Prev. 3rd St., on Gunter Annex of Maxwell AFB, renamed to recognize Pvt. Frederick Libby, who was the first American to down five enemy aircraft during World War I. He had 10 "kills" as an enlisted man and was honored by King George V at Buckingham Palace. He was commissioned later and downed 14 more aircraft as an officer.

Liberty Street

The name was probably influenced by patriotic feelings during WWI.

Lichfield Court

See Wynlakes.

Liles Court

Montgomery developer and contractor Duncan Liles.

Lilly Lane

Developed by William Thames and named for his daughter.

Limestone Court

A hard rock formed from deposits of organic matter. County organized in 1818 and named for Limestone Creek. Parallel to Cobblestone and Sandstone courts.

Lincoln Road, Street, Terrace

Rd: Located near an old cemetery of the same name. St., Terr.: Possibly for Gen. Benjamin Lincoln (1773-1810), a Revolutionary War hero for whom a town in Talladega County is named; cities in Neb. and Ill.

Linda Circle (E. & W.), Lane †

Linden Street

Possibly related to the town in Marengo County whose name is derived from *Hohenlinden* in honor of the victory of the

French Gen. Moreau over the Austrian forces of Archduke John at Hohenlinden in Bavaria in 1800. The town was incorporated in 1823.

Lisa Court
Named by developer William K. Thames, Sr., for the granddaughter of former Auburn Coach, the late Ralph "Shug" Jordan.

Little Lane
Raymond L. Little, former owner of the Downtowner Motor Inn.

Little John Court, Drive
Named for the character in the Robin Hood legend and located in the Forest Hills Subdivision.

Livebrook Lane
See Brookview Manor.

Live Oak Court
A majestic, long-lived tree growing in this neighborhood; near White Oak La.

Lizmar Lane
Elizabeth Mary Thames, the daughter of developer David Thames.

Liztame Drive
Elizabeth Whetstone Thames, the wife of developer William K. Thames, Sr.

Llanfair Road
Welsh for "fair church," located in a British-themed area.

Lloyd Street
See Capitol Heights.

Llyde Lane
The mother of developer William K. Thames, Sr.

Loch Haven Road
See "Montgomery's Own Philadelphia Story."

Lochwood Drive
See Wynlakes.

Lockerbie Street
A city in Scotland.

Lockett Drive
One of a series of streets in the Lee High School area named

by 1920s developers for women's names, natural features and family names.

Lockridge Road
A street in Woodley Meadows located closest to Whites Slough.

Locust Street
See Oak Park.

Loisa Lane †

Lola Lane †

Lomac Street
A combination of the first names of two children in the Seth Johnson family. See Seth Johnson Dr.

Lombard Drive
See "Montgomery's Own Philadelphia Story."

London Road
A Carol Villa street probably named by newer developers than the Johnson family, who were the original land owners.

London House Road
See Brookview Manor.

Lone Oak Drive
For a prominent oak tree in Prairie View Estates.

Lonesome Pine Drive
Located in the Dannelly Pines neighborhood.

Longbrook Drive
See Brookview Manor.

Longleaf Drive
Located in the Dannelly Pines neighborhood.

Longmeadow Drive
A pleasant name that evokes rural beauty.

Longneedle Drive, Place
See Wynlakes.

Long Ridge Road
A short street along a ridge. See Fox Hollow.

Longview Court, Street
J. R. Long, a former property owner on that block.

Lookout Ridge Road
Located in the hilly Mountain View Estates subdivision.

Lorenzo Street †

Loring Street †

Lorraine Street †

Lott Drive
Eugene Lott Hill, a son of Luther Leonidas Hill.

Louis Street
Possibly for Louis Loeb, an area property developer in the 1880s and 1890s.

Louisville Street
Parallels the railroad of the same name.

Louis Armstrong Park

Situated immediately west of the official entrance to Capitol Heights, at the corner of Madison Terr. and Madison Ave., Louis Armstrong Park stands on the former homestead of James Steptoe Pinckard, one of the primary developers of Capitol Heights. After Pinckard's home was destroyed by fire, the city of Montgomery bought this property for "an amazingly small sum of money"—$45,000, to be exact—and decided to build a park on the lot.

During the debate over the name for the park, the community residents voiced opinions about naming the park after the original owner of the land to honor him and preserve the history of the area. However, at the ribbon-cutting ceremony, residents learned that the park had been named Louis Armstrong Park rather than the favored Pinckard Park.

The park is named for Louis Armstrong, of Montgomery, the long-time minister of Morningview Baptist Church and chaplain of the Robert E. Lee High School football team.

Loveless Curve †

Lowell Street †

Lower Wetumpka Road

One of two roads to Wetumpka. It is called "lower" because of its relation to the Upper Wetumpka Rd. and is more susceptible to flooding.

Lowes Court

For the Lowes hardware store now relocated several miles up the Eastern Bypass.

Lowry Street

See Capitol Heights.

Loxley Lane

Named for the Robin Hood legend and located in Forest Hills.

Lucas Street

See King's Hill. Of interest: Henry Lucas, one of the area's early emigrants, owned the area formerly known as Old Augusta on the Tallapoosa River. The site was once the Indian village, Souvanogee, and the home of Tecumseh's parents before they were removed to Ohio.

Lucian Lane

Probably a family name important to the development of Garden Square.

Lucy Street †

Lunceford Street

For real estate developer Tommy Lunsford, whose name is misspelled in some uses.

Lurene Circle

The wife of area landowner Wiley Pearson Johnson.

Luther Drive

Honoring Dr. Martin Luther King, Jr., near Coretta Dr. in Twin Gates. King was shot while standing on the balcony of his motel room in Memphis, Tenn., on April 4, 1968. The civil rights leader once said, "Nothing in the world is more dangerous than sincere ignorance."

Luverne Street

Wife of M. P. LeGrand, a real estate promoter. The county seat of Crenshaw County was named for her also.

Luxembourg Circle

See Halcyon.

Lycoming Court, Road
A college in Williamsport, Penn., founded in 1812.

Lyerly Lane
See Highland Gardens.

Lyman Court †

Lynchburg Court (E. & W.), Drive
In a neighborhood with other Va. references.

Lyndle Road †

Lynnhurst Court, Lane
Possibly for the decendants of Major General Phineas Lyman, recipient of a royal land-grant in the Miss. Territory in 1773.

Lynton Drive
Lynton Caldwell, an owner of the land.

Lynwood Drive
Lyn Weinstein, the son of Les Weinstein.

M

Mabson Drive
Ben Mabson, a state consulting engineer.

Mace Avenue †

Macedonia Drive
In the neighborhood of Macedonia, home to Macedonia Baptist Church.

MacLamar Road
Possibly a combination of two names.

Madison Avenue, Terrace
Ave.: James Madison (1751-1836), fourth president of the U.S. Terr.: prev. Vickers St. The section known as King's Hill was still called Vickers St. as late as 1948. See Van Allen Dr.

Madolyn Lane
See Forest Hills.

Maggie Street
In a neighborhood of first names used for streets.

Magnolia Avenue, Boulevard, Curve
A fragrant flowering tree often symbolic of the deep South; see Highland Park, Maxwell AFB and Cloverdale. Of inter-

est: On April 12, 1854, former President Millard Fillmore visited the city, arriving aboard a steamship bearing the same name.

Major Street
In a neighborhood of streets using proper names with British connotations. See Kenilworth St.

Malabar Road
A city in southwest India, bordering the Arabian Sea.

Mallard Court, Lane
See Twin Lakes Pkwy.

Mallory Street
One of a series of streets in the Lee High School area named by 1920s developers for women's names, natural features and family names.

Malone Drive
Possibly related to a community in Randolph County established in 1908, and probably named for a family there.

Malvern Street
A town in Geneva County named in honor of the Civil War Battle of Malvern Hill in Va.

Manasse Drive
Civil War buff C. T. Fitzpatrick named this street for the battles of Manassas.

Manchester Drive
Located in an area of English-themed names.

Mangrove Lane
A tropical evergreen tree or shrub that grows densely along tidal shores. Located in Sunshine Acres.

Manley Drive
Probably a family name important to the development of Garden Square.

Mansfield Drive
In a neighborhood of streets with proper names.

Maple Street
See Maxwell AFB, Oak Park. A prolific tree species grown for shade, timber and its sap, which is used for syrup.

Maple Ridge Lane
See Sturbridge.

March Road, Street

These two streets are on Maxwell AFB, and one of them memorializes 2nd Lt. Peyton Conway March, Jr. He enlisted in the U.S. Army in 1917 and was assigned to the aviation section. He was mortally wounded in an airplane crash at San Antonio (Feb. 1918) and died the following month. His father was Chief of Staff of the U.S. Army during WWI, and may be for whom the other street was designated.

Marco Road

A proper name or possibly a reference to Marco Polo, explorer of the Orient.

Margaret Ann Drive

The daughter of Don Martin, a local real estate developer.

Margo Place

Retired Col. Hugh Hughes, a West Point graduate employed by Ballard Realty for 20 years, gave several streets in the Woodmere subdivision feminine German names. See Astrid Pl., Greta Pl., Heidi Pl. and Helga Pl.

Marguerite Street

One of a series of streets named for females in the Bel Air development that was owned by A.G. Tuttle in the 1880s. Of interest: Marguerite is the heroine of Gounod's popular opera *Faust*, which premiered in New York in 1883.

Marie Cook Drive

Wife of James H. Cook, who, along with George Laurie, bought the Dalraida area land from a Ware family descendent in 1909. John H. Haardt developed the property for Mrs. Cook and named the street in her honor.

Market Place

Located in a business area.

Marlborough Street

A town in England located south of Birmingham; an English royal dukedom; and also a brand of smoking tobacco. Situated in an area of streets named for cigarettes and parallel to Salem and Kent streets.

Marlowe Drive

A famous playwright and poet of Elizabethan England, in an area of English-themed names.

Marlyn Street †

Marquette Drive

An early French explorer. See "Montgomery's Own Philadelphia Story."

Marshall Street

A county in north Ala. named for John Marshall (1755-1835), the fourth chief justice of the U.S. Supreme Court.

Marsh Pointe Drive

Located in a marshy area.

Martha Street

George Root Clayton married a woman named Martha. This street, part of the original Clayton plat, was probably named for her.

Marti Lane

Bud Chamber's daughter.

Martin Street

See Jackson Ferry Pk.

Martin Luther King, Jr., Expressway

Named in honor of the slain civil rights leader who began his career in Montgomery in 1954. The resolution designating a section of I-85 as the MLK Expressway was passed by the Alabama Legislature in 1976. This action followed the failure of a racially divided Montgomery City Council to agree on a local ordinance that would have renamed Jackson Street— where King lived during his Montgomery years—as as a memorial to King. See Luther Dr.

Martin Patton Street

In an area where people's names are used for streets.

Mary Street

Named as part of the Ford property developed in 1893.

Mary Ann Drive

In a neighborhood of first and last names used for streets. Near Mary Ethel Dr.

Mary Ethel Drive

In a neighborhood of first and last names used for streets. Near Mary Ann Dr.

Mary F. Terrell Street

Mary Frances Terrell taught English at her *alma mater*, the State Normal School, for 51 years. She was responsible for initiating a birthday tribute for the school's president, William Burns Paterson, which evolved into the current Founder's Day celebration at Alabama State University. A building named for her was demolished in the early 1970s, and a campus street was designated in her honor in 1974.

Maryland Drive (N. & S.), Street

The state of Md.; state names used in Capitol Heights, where street is located.

Mary Lou Lane †

Mason Avenue, Street

Ave.: Family name of the original Carol Villa landowner Seth Johnson's wife, Neva Kate Carmichael's grandmother. St.: Named by D. S. Troy in 1870.

Mastin Lane

For Peter B. Mastin, who settled on Ramer Creek in 1834. He made himself wealthy by grinding corn and sawing lumber at a mill that he built on the creek. In 1851 he purchased lands of the Fairview plantation and "built a fine residence."

Matterhorn Court, Street

Ironically, although this street is flat, it is named for the famous peak in the Pennine Alps on the Italian-Swiss border.

Maury Street

Possibly for Matthew Fontaine Maury, director of U.S. Naval Observatory from 1844-61.

Maxwell AFB

The streets and avenues on Maxwell AFB and Gunter Annex were originally given Arabic numerals, letters of the alphabet or names of trees. This practice facilitates the renaming of the streets to memoralize deserving individuals as determined by an appropriate board. The board is convened as necessary to consider individuals who have been nominated for this honor. Buildings, parks and other facilities on the base are similarly named.

Maxwell Avenue, Boulevard

Ave.: Located just south of Maxwell AFB and probably named for the base rather than the man. See Maxwell AFB. Blvd.: A principal thoroughfare on Maxwell AFB, this street originates at the main gate on Bell St. and proceeds northwest into the heart of the base. It was designated to memorialize 1st Lt. William Calvin Maxwell, who grew up in Atmore. He enlisted in the U.S. Army in May 1917, was commissioned as 2nd Lt. in April 1918, and served during WWI. He was sent to the Philippines in 1920. In August, he experienced engine problems and attempted to land his aircraft on a sugar plantation. Prior to touchdown, he noticed children playing and swerved the plane to avoid hitting them. He hit a flag pole instead and was killed instantly.

May Street †

Mayfair Drive

A district in London where fairs were held during the 17th century. The district later became a tony residential area but is now used primarily for offices. In an area of English-themed names.

Mayflower Road

The ship that brought the pilgrims to Mass. in 1620 and gave its name to the Mayflower Compact, the first self-governance agreement in the New World.

McCain Lane †

McCampbell Drive †

McCarter Avenue

See Capitol Heights.

McChord Street †

McCracken Avenue

Prev. Avenue D, on Gunter Annex of Maxwell AFB, renamed to honor 2nd Lt. Murro A. McCracken, who was the fourth American to die in an aircraft accident while stationed at Gunter Field in 1941.

McCurdy Street

Louis A. McCurdy, a vice-president of the Southern United Life Insurance Co.

McDonald Street

Prev. 5th St., renamed in honor of Sgt. William C. McDonald, a member of the famous "Men on the Flying Trapeze," an aero demonstration team established at Maxwell Field in 1934 by Capt. Claire Chennault. Sgt. McDonald was also a member of the "Flying Tigers," a group of Americans recruited to fly for the Chinese during WWII. The street is located on Gunter Annex of Maxwell AFB.

McDonough Street (N. & S.)
War of 1812 Naval Commodore Thomas Macdonough, the hero of Lake Champlain, where he defeated the British when they attempted to attack New York. His name is actually spelled "Macdonough," but histories have consistently used the spelling preserved in this street name. It was one of the last streets in the downtown area to be paved because it was used to drive cattle to market until the 1920s.

McElvy Street
Liles McElvy, a local developer and contractor.

McGehee Place
Street names in this development were randomly chosen from the Tuscaloosa city directory.

McGehee Place Court, Drive (N. & S.); McGehee Road
For Boyd and Hardie McGehee, brothers who operated the largest drug store in Montgomery and also owned the land. Abner McGehee, a nephew of John Scott, founded the Alabama Bible Society, the oldest Christian bookstore in America. It has been at its present location since 1852.

McGinnis Street
In an area of last names used for streets.

McGowan Street
In an area of last names used for streets near the heart of Cottage Hill.

McGraw Court
H. D. McGraw.

McHugh Alley
In an area of last names used for streets.

McInnis Drive, Road
Probably named for McInnis School, serving handicapped youth, founded in early 1950s by the McInnis family along with others. The family also owned a large dairy farm in the area.

McIntire Court

LeRoy and Vivian McIntire. He is the stepson of W. Inge Hill, Sr., the owner of the land at the time of its development.

McKinley Avenue

William McKinley, the 25th president of the U.S. (1897-1901), who took America into the popular Spanish-American War.

McKinney Street †

McMillan Street

The owner or developer of this property.

McNarney Street

Prev. 12th St., on Maxwell AFB, honors Gen. Joseph T. McNarney, who served in WWI and WWII. During WWII, he was appointed Deputy Supreme Allied Commander in the Mediterranean Theatre, CG of the U.S. Army Forces, CG of the U.S. Forces in Europe, and Commander in charge of U.S. Forces of Occupation in Germany. During his lengthy service in the two wars, he was awarded five Distinguished Service medals, the Legion of Merit, the Navy DSM, and decorations from Great Britain, Yugoslavia, Chile, Brazil, Italy, France, Belgium, Poland, Czechoslovakia and the USSR.

McQueen Street

One of a series of streets in the Lee High School area named by 1920s developers for women's names, natural features and family names.

Meadow Lane

Overlooks the Colonial Acres Country Club.

Meadowbriar Court

In Woodley Meadows, one of several landscape-themed names.

Meadowlane Drive

Located near the Montgomery Country Club.

Meadow Lark Drive

In the blackbird family, valued because it eats insect pests and has a beautiful song.

Meadow Oak Court

See Halcyon.

Meadowridge Lane
The ridge of a meadow that now overlooks the Ala. Shakespeare Festival.

Meadow View Street
Former meadow land.

Meadow Walk Lane, Court
Former meadow, now adjacent to an existing meadow.

Medford Court, Lane
The name of cities in Mass. and Ore.

Meehan Street †

Melanie Drive
A Carol Villa street probably named by later developers and not the Johnson family, original landowners.

Melrose Street
The Scottish birthplace of James Davidson, who immigrated to Montgomery in 1849. He was the city treasurer and supporter of the Highland Park development. See Highland Park. Of note: The old Melrose Hotel was located on Church St. during the 1930s.

Melton Road, Street
Rd.: Melton Hill Tankersley, Will Hill Tankersley's brother. St.: See Kenilworth St.

Mendel Parkway (E. & W.)
Perry Mendel, former executive of Kinder-Care.

Menlo Court
Menlo Park, N.J., was the site of Thomas Edison's experimental laboratory. The light bulb was invented there in 1879.

Meredith Drive
In an area of women's first names for streets.

Meridian Lane
This neighborhood's section line is close to a prime meridian, an imaginary graphic line drawn as a great circle, which crosses parallels of latitude and the North and South Poles.

Meriwether Circle, Road
For Benjamin Baldwin Meriwether, whose ancestor, Dr. Nicholas Meriwether, was the recipient of an original land grant from Andrew Jackson. See Halcyon.

Merrily Drive
In an area of women's first names used for several streets.

Merrimac Court, Drive

The ironclad *Merrimac* (renamed the *Virginia)* fought the *Monitor* in Hampton Roads, Va., during the Civil War in 1862.

Merritt Court

Jerry Merritt, a local banker.

Michael Street

Named as part of the S. M. Simpson subdivision in 1907.

Michelle Court

A Carol Villa street probably named by newer developers than the Johnson family, original landowners.

Michigan Avenue, Court

The state of Mich.

Middlefork Road

See Young Place.

Midfield Drive

Formerly farmland.

Midlane Court

Located at a midpoint between Carter Hill Rd. and Fairview Ave. on Narrow Lane Rd.

Midpark Road

Bisects Gunter Industrial Park. See Gunter Park Dr. E.

Mid Pines Drive

See Wynlakes.

Midway Court, Street

The center of Highland Gardens.

Milan Court, Drive

A city in Italy.

Mildred Street

A daughter in the Clayton family, prominent early Montgomerians.

Miles Street

In an area of surnames for streets, developed in the 1920s.

Mill Street

In an area developing in the late 1800s, when a mill probably stood nearby.

Miller Street

Named by Fred Cramton, the developer of Highland Gardens, for his friends E. B. Miller and Clara E. Miller, former owners of this property. See Cramton Bowl and Highland Gardens.

Mill Ridge Court, Drive
See Halcyon.

Millstone Court
In the old Norris Farms area, where on the creek a mill might once have served the local community.

Millwood Court
A Carol Villa street probably named by newer developers than the Johnson family, original landowners.

Milton Road †

Mimosa Drive, Road
A pink-flowering tree popular in this area. See also Maxwell AFB.

Miriam Street
See Capitol Heights.

Mitchell Avenue, Street
Ave.: One of three parallel streets with proper names. St.: Prev. 3rd St., on Maxwell AFB, redesignated to honor Maj. Gen. William "Billy" Mitchell. Mitchell and Charles Lindbergh are the only two airmen ever to receive the Medal of Honor in peacetime. Mitchell is best remembered, however, as a prophet of American air power and for his outspoken criticism of military officials and others who did not share his beliefs in air excellence and potential. His frank fault-finding earned the animosity of his superiors and resulted in a general court-martial in 1925. He was found guilty and suspended from rank and duty with no pay and allowances for five years. President Coolidge confirmed the sentence in 1926, and Mitchell resigned from the army. He died 10 years later. In 1947, Congress passed a special bill promoting him to major general retroactive to the date of his death. Another Mitchell St. in Dalraida probably bears a local family name.

Mitzi Court
In an area of women's first names used for streets.

Mobile Drive, Highway, Road, Street
From the Indian name "Maubila," the name of a tribe living below the formation of the Mobile River that took this name from a term taken to mean "the rowers." Dr.: Parallels Mo-

bile Hwy. and bisects the Mobile Heights neighborhood. Hwy, Rd., St.: Former routes south to Mobile. Hwy: U.S.Hwy. 31, which runs from the Alabama-Tennessee state line to Mobile.

Mohawk Drive
Iroquoian-speaking North American tribe, the easternmost group of the Iroquoian League.

Molton Street
Thomas Molton, an early planter in Montgomery County.

Mona Lisa Drive
A famous portrait painted by Leonardo Da Vinci.

Monette Street
Located in an area of last names used for streets.

Money Road
John Money, a local business owner.

Monmouth Mews
A mews is a small street or alley on which a stable or outbuilding stands. See Halcyon.

Monroe Street
James Monroe (1758-1831), the fifth president of the U.S.

Montclair Drive
See Chisholm.

Monterey Court, Drive
Cities in Mexico and California bear this Spanish name. See Monterey Park.

■ MONTEREY PARK
An area developed with a Spanish theme.

Montero Drive
In an area of Spanish themes. "Montero," derived from the Spanish word for mountain, refers to a hunter and his cap with side flaps.

Montezuma Road
For the Aztec emperor, Montezuma.

Montgomery Street
City and county. The city was named for Gen. Richard Montgomery (1736-1775), who was killed in the Battle of Quebec in 1775. The county was named for Maj. Lemuel P. Montgomery, who was killed in the Battle of Horseshoe Bend by

Creek Indians. The street is also the site of the historic Empire, reputed to be the world's first air-conditioned theatre.

Monticello Court, Drive, Road
The estate of Thomas Jefferson near Charlottesville, Va.

Montreat Drive
A Presbyterian retreat in N.C.

Montrose Avenue
A city in Great Britain, in an area with a British motif.

Montview Court
A combination of "Montgomery" and "view."

Mont Vista Drive
See "Montgomery's Own Philadelphia Story."

Montwood Court, Drive
A combination of "Montgomery" and "wood."

Moorcroft Drive
In a British-themed area. A moor is a high plateau, and a croft is a small enclosed pasture or farm.

Moore Drive
On Gunter Annex of Maxwell AFB, the street probably honors Maj. Gen. Thomas Estes Moore, who was the director of USAF planning during the 1960s.

Mooreland Road †

Morgan Avenue
Probably for John Tyler Morgan, a prominent U.S. Senator and CSA general. Possibly for James Augustus Morgan, a teacher educated at Ross College who taught in Roanoke and resided in Lincoln (Roanoke, Ross and Lincoln are names of relatively nearby streets). Possibly for Morgan County, organized in 1818 and named for Gen. Daniel Morgan of Va.

Morning Glory Court
In a neighborhood with botanical street names.

Morning Mist
In an area whose street names evoke country scenes and places.

Morningview Street
Near Morningview School and Morningview Baptist Church, in an area said to have been generally known by that name.

Morris Avenue (S.), Street
Ave: Prev. Avenue A, on Gunter Annex of Maxwell AFB, renamed to honor 2nd Lt. F.H. Morris, the first American to

die in an aircraft accident while stationed at Gunter Field, in 1941. St.: Josiah Morris, prominent 19th-century Montgomery banker who financed the Elyton Land Co.'s purchase of 4,150 acres to be the site of a town that he named Birmingham after the industrial city in England.

Mose Street †

Moses Street
Owners of the Moses Brothers Co. and property owners in late 1800s.

Mosswood
A subdivision with a foliage theme.

Mosswood Road
See Mosswood.

Mossy Glen Road
Descriptive of the rural area recently developed.

Mossy Oak Drive
Located in a thoroughly forested area.

Motley Road †

Mountainview Drive
Located in the hilly Mountainview Estates subdivision.

Moye Drive (E. & N.)
Mary Louise Moye, the former daughter-in-law of Montgomery developer William K. Thames, Sr.

Mt. Meigs Road
Led from 19th-century Montgomery east to Mt. Meigs, the settlement that was first called Evansville and later Mt. Pleasant. It now bears the name of a family who ran a store and gin there.

Mt. Vernon Drive
First U.S. president George Washington's home in Alexandria, Va.

Mulberry Street
See Highland Park.

Mulligan Drive
In an area of British-themed names; this is an Irish surname.

Mulzer Boulevard
In an area of last names used for streets.

Murray Street

See King's Hill. A second Murray St. is in an area of last names used for streets that came into the city in 1910 and probably honors James Murray, who was the clerk for the Western Railroad (Montgomery to Selma) during the late 1800s.

Museum Drive

Location of the Montgomery Museum of Fine Arts. See "Wynton M. Blount Cultural Park."

Myles Street

Named as part of the S. M. Simpson subdivision in 1907.

Myrtle Street

Situated in Cottage Hills, one of several streets named for women.

Myrtlewood Drive

Crape myrtle is a popular shrub in the South; this area is marked by garden and plant references.

N

Nancy Court

In an area with several men's and women's first names for streets.

Narrow Lane Court, Road, Parkway

Originally a dirt lane not wide enough for two wagons to pass each other.

Nash Street

J. G. Nash, former president of Judson College (1864-65).

Nassau Avenue

A popular Caribbean tourist spot. The street is intersected by Riviera Rd.

Natchez Court, Drive

An Indian tribe related to the Muskhogean. See Arrowhead.

National Street

This area came into the city after WWI.

Nature Court, Drive

Near Eden Dr. and separated by railroad tracks.

Navajo Drive

An Indian tribe originating in Canada that settled in the

Southwest. See Arrowhead.

Navarro Street

Possibly for Pedro Navarro, a conquistador and Spanish official in Florida in the early 1500s.

Neely Lane †

Neese Drive

Larry Neese, an area realtor.

Neill Drive †

Nesbitt Avenue

In an area of people's last names used for streets.

Nevem Drive

A combination of the names of the sixth and eighth child (out of 12) of Carol Villa land owner Seth Johnson, Neva Carmichael and Emily Katherine.

Newbury Lane

A city in Mass.

Newby Court †

Newcastle Lane

A short name for Newcastle upon Tyne, the site of a Roman military station and later coal-shipping port. The phrase "to carry coals to Newcastle" means to do something not needed.

Newcomb Avenue †

Newell Parkway

Honors W. S. "Buffalo Bill" Newell, a prominent businessman and civic leader who is known by many children in the area as the man who has buffalo grazing on the grounds of his estate located on Bell Rd.

Newport Road

A summer center for America's Gilded Age rich, Newport, R.I.

Nickel Street

Lewis Nickel, the owner of the property.

Nicrosi Street

Prev. Sternfield Alley. William B. Nicrosi, Sr., a local developer and realtor, developed nearby Paterson Court, Montgomery's first housing project.

Ninth Street

One of three streets in a series of numbered streets including only 6th, 8th and 9th streets.

Noble Avenue

For George D. Noble, the property owner in the 1890s. Of interest: George W. Noble was the first city treasurer after Montgomery was chartered as a city on Dec. 23, 1837.

Noble Wood Court

See Halcyon.

Nora Place

Retired Col. Hugh Hughes, a West Point graduate employed by Ballard Realty, gave several steets in Woodmere feminine German names.

Nordale Drive

A combination of "Norman" and "dale" in "Normandale."

Nordan Lane

For Curtis Nordan, Sr., an area Realtor.

Noremac Road

This is developer John Cameron's last name spelled backwards.

■ NORMANDALE

See "Normandale."

Norman Lane

Off of Norman Bridge Rd., this street is part of the southern boundary of Normandale. See "Normandale."

Norman Bridge Court, Road

Job Norman, 7 feet tall and weighing 400 pounds, built the first bridge over Catoma Creek on property where Norman Bridge Rd. begins in order to visit the Waller family, who lived on Waller Creek in the mid-19th century. See "Normandale."

Normandie Drive

French spelling of Normandy, the historic region in France that was the site of the first step in the Allied invasion of Europe.

Norris Drive

A family name that is important to the development of Garden Square.

Norris Farms Road

Farm land once owned by Roger C. Norris.

Normandale

The concept of creating a self-contained neighborhood was born in Montgomery with Normandale. Developed by Aronov Realty, it has since served as a model for others throughout the nation. Planning started in 1952, and the shopping center opened in Sept. 1954. The modern-looking, spacious shopping center, one of the first malls in America, attracted attention by its placement on a thoroughfare, Norman Bridge Rd. (from which it took its name). Both apartments and homes provided housing around the shopping center, and its streets were curved so as to vary the view from any one vantage point. Lots were set aside for churches and other services so that the community would be complete. Normandale is located about three miles south of the heart of downtown, and at the time of its opening was one of the most sought-after addresses despite the distance.

Cloverland Shopping Center and residential area were also developed at about the same time, spurring growth to the south side of the city.

During this time, Joe Sadler, a post office superintendent, was busy fighting "off a plague" of duplicate street names and numbers caused by the new developments in the fast-growing city. He sponsored an ordinance to eliminate duplicate names. The city took it a step farther and also eliminated duplicate numbers. To avoid these problems, Aaron Aronov called Sadler for help with the Normandale area, saying he wanted some "good-sounding" names. Sadler said, for example, that he picked Bridlewood Dr. because the Normandale area had once been a great farm. "Why not?" he said.

North Drive, Street

Dr: Runs from east to west near the northern boundary of Gunter Annex of Maxwell AFB. St.: Part of James B. Copeland's development in 1866, located north of Center St. and South St. (no longer in existence.)

North Belt Drive

Prev. Waste Way, for transfer station of Waste Away, Inc., but changed when a drag racing track was established there in 1995.

North Chase Boulevard

Off Northern Blvd.

Northfield Drive

See Young Place.

Northgate Drive

Northgate housing project is located just south of this area.

North Gap Loop/North Pass Road

Located off of the Northern Bypass, in a neighborhood called North Pass.

Northern Boulevard

A section of the perimeter circle around the city from I-65 to U.S. 231 N. This busy route was originally intended to by-pass the city.

North Valley Road

In the North Pass area.

Northwestern Road

A university in Evanston, Ill., founded in 1851. See College Grove.

Norwich Drive

A borough of eastern England northeast of London and a city in southeast Conn.

Norwood Street

Probably for Joseph Norwood (1854-1919), vice president of the Exchange National Bank in Montgomery and state senator in 1903.

Nottingham Court, Road

Named for the Robin Hood legend and located in the Forest Hills subdivision.

O

Oak Alley, Avenue, Street

Alley: In Wynlakes, named for a Mississippi plantation. Ave.: One of three parallel streets named for trees—Oak, Cedar and Elm— bisected by Orchard Ave. St.: There are several streets with this name in different neighborhoods. A tree of the beech family bearing the acorn as fruit, which produces durable wood used in furniture making. See Maxwell AFB.

Oakbrook Court, Drive

See Brookview Manor.

Oakdale Drive

In an area of tree and shrub names used for streets.

Oak Forest Drive

One of a series of streets in the Lee High School area named by 1920s developers for women's names, natural features and family names.

Oakland Street

Named by W. C. Holt in his Kensington suburb in 1891.

Oakleigh Road

See Regency Park.

Oak Meadow Court

See Sturbridge.

Oak Park

See Highland Park.

Oak Ridge Court

So named for the multitude of trees in the area. See Forest Hills.

Oak Shadow Court, Lane

See Carriage Hills.

Oakview Court (N. & S.)

Another area of Montgomery where oaks abound.

Oakwild Court, Drive

An area of wild forests before its development in the 1960s.

Ocala Court, Drive

Derived from "Ocali," an obscure Indian word possibly referring to an ancient Timucuan province or the middle part of Florida.

O'Connell Street
John C. O'Connell, a property developer in the late 19th century.

Ogden Avenue (E. & W.)
In an area of last names used for streets.

Oglethorpe Road
James Oglethorpe founded the colony of Georgia in 1733. See also "Montgomery's Own Philadelphia Story."

Oklahoma Street
For the state of Okla., and located a few blocks from Kansas St.

Old Barn Road
See Arrowhead West.

Old Cahaba Road
The French founded Cahaba (near the river of that name) as a trading post on a grant from Louis XV. It was Alabama's capital city 1819-26, but abandoned because of floods and disease. Today ghostly street markers lay out what once was a fine city.

Oldcastle Place
Sir John Oldcastle, a friend of Henry V of England, who was immortalized as John Falstaff in Shakespeare's history plays. See "Wynton M. Blount Cultural Park."

Old Creek Court, Road
In a neighborhood with several references to waterways.

Old Dobbin Road
A horse, especially a workhorse. Derivative of "dobbin" as an alteration of "robin." See Carriage Hills.

Old Farm Road
A former farm site. See also Young Farm.

Old Federal Road
A road from Washington to New Orleans traveled by pioneers in the early 1800s, which came into Montgomery from Mt. Meigs and left the city heading southwest toward Mobile. Lafayette used this road when he visited the city in 1825, and a few traces of it remain. See "The Old Federal Road."

Oldfield Circle, Court, Drive, Place
See Arrowhead West.

The Old Federal Road

The area's first road was built in 1805-06, despite protests from native Creek Indians. The Old Federal Road entered east Alabama at Fort Mitchell and continued west, roughly parallel to the current U. S. Highway 80, and continued to Mt. Meigs. Soon after passing Lucas' Tavern, the road turned south, following the Alamuchee-Creek trail, and traversed what is now the Halcyon neighborhood, crossing Vaughn Road, Bell Road, and the Troy Highway, and continued through the middle of Snowdoun to Marengo County and on to Mobile.

Intended as a mail route from Washington, D.C., to New Orleans, the road was maintained by the Indians, who were paid $1,200 per year for their labor. The road soon became the prime route for migration to and through Alabama. Resourceful Indians took advantage of the traffic by erecting roadside "stands" to market their wares and produce. Settlements grew up at these sites, and some, Warrior Stand in Macon County, for example, still exist.

Although the route was considered fairly safe after the Battle of Horseshoe Bend, travel along the Old Federal Road was arduous, and many who died along the way were buried where they fell. Thus, old cemeteries and single graves mark the route. One grave at La Place Church is that of George Stiggins, noted for writing a history of his people—the Creek Indians—in the early 1800s.

The road fell into disuse during the 1830s or 1840s, probably because of the improved river travel and competition from other roads, such as Three Notch Road, constructed in 1824. Portions of the original road survive near Pintlala and in the Wyndridge neighborhood. They still bear the name—Old Federal Road.

Old Forest Court, Road
See Arrowhead West.

Old Hayneville Road
Hayneville is a community S.W. of Montgomery that has been reached by this route from the time in the 1820s when it was known as "Big Swamp." Named for Robert C. Hayne, a former governor of N.C.

Old Lake Road
See Arrowhead West.

Old Lamar Road
Harold Lamar, an area landowner.

Old Leeds Road
Leeds, a metropolitan area of West Yorkshire, England.

Old Magnolia Way
See Sturbridge.

Old Marsh Way
See Wynlakes.

Old Mill Court
An extension of the creek theme used in this area.

Old Orchard Lane
Miles of orchards and farms dotted the eastern trip out of Montgomery along Vaughn Rd., so it is likely that this was indeed orchard land.

Old Pond Road
Near Old Creek, Fox Creek, Cherry Creek and other similar references.

Old Post Lane
In an area of horse-racing themes for streets.

Old Powder Spring Road
A spring likely helped to feed the nearby slough and led to the waterway references used frequently in this area.

Old Pump Court, Place, Road
See Arrowhead West.

Old Savannah Lane
See Sturbridge.

Old Selma Road
The original route from Montgomery to Selma, a town located on the Alabama River in Dallas County. William Rufus

King picked the town's name from the *Poems of Ossian*, by James MacPherson.

Old Shell Road

This road was once covered with oyster shells discarded by restaurants. It becomes McDonough St. as it crosses railroad tracks into Montgomery.

Old Thorington Road

See Thorington St.

Old Wetumpka Highway, Road

A meeting of the stockholders of the Montgomery and Pickett Springs Gravel Road Co. in 1869 resulted in appointing a committee to extend this road from Montgomery to Wetumpka.

Olive Street

See Oak Park and Maxwell AFB.

Oliver Court, Drive, Road

Dr. Thomas Winfrey Oliver, a native of Snowdoun, began farming near what was then the Brown Plantation (of Brown's Spring Rd. area). He married Thomas Brown's granddaughter in 1854.

Olivia Court

One of a series of streets in the Lee High School area named by 1920s developers for women's names, natural features and family names.

Opp Street

Henry Opp, a lawyer and the principal promoter of a settlement by that name in S. Ala.

Orchard Avenue

Bisects three parallel avenues named for trees—Oak, Cedar and Elm.

Oriole Drive

A colorful orange-marked bird, the official bird of Md.

Orlando Drive

A south-central Fla. city. The title of a book by Virginia Woolf, which first appeared in 1928.

Orum Street †

Otis Lane

In a neighborhood of names used for streets.

Ousley Street
Possibly Clarence Newdaygate Ousley, a former U.S. assistant secretary of agriculture.

Overhill Road
At the edge of Meadow La., overlooking rolling countryside.

Overlook Drive
The street ends on a bluff overlooking a "prong" of Three Mile Creek.

Owen Court †

Owens Street
Named as part of The Uplands, a subdivision developed by Joseph Lee Rhodes of the West Virginia Land Co. in 1906.

Oxford Drive
Honors Oxford University in England.

Oxmoor Lane †

P

Paddock Lane
See County Downs.

Page Place
Martha Page Fitzpatrick (Mrs.C. T. Fitzpatrick).

Palma Drive
City on Majorca Island in Spain, in the Bay of Palma.

Palmetto Street
Small palms with fan-shaped leaves. See Oak Park.

Pama Court †

Pamela Court
Near Carol and Mitzi, in a neighborhood of streets with people's first names.

Pampas Court, Drive, Place, Point
Treeless plains of South America, south of the Amazon.

Panama Street (N. & S.)
The Panama Canal is mentioned in a promotional pamphlet about Capitol Heights, describing the South as a center of potential industrial and commercial growth.

Parallel Street

Parallel to Louisville and Nashville R.R.

Park Avenue (E. & W.), Boulevard, Place

Avenues: off Lower Wetumpka Rd.; also in Cloverdale and Chisholm; Blvd: In Executive Park; Pl.: Runs into Oak Park.

Parker Lane, Street †

Park Manor Avenue, Drive (W.)

Located in the Park Manor neighborhood.

Park Towne Way (S.)

The site of the Park Towne Apartments.

Parkview Drive (S.)

See Wynlakes.

Parkwood Court, Drive

A town near Durham, N.C., an area where many local developers maintained summer homes.

Partridge Road

C. T. Fitzpatrick, a sportsman, named this after the fowl.

Patio Place

See "Montgomery's Own Philadelphia Story."

Patricia Lane

In a neighborhood with several women's first names used for streets.

Patrick Court (E.), Road, Street

Ct.: New street in Halcyon. Rd. and St.: In areas of first names used for streets.

Patterson Road †

Patton Avenue

Honors Gen. George S. Patton (1885-1945), the American WWII commander. After surviving WWI and WWII, he was killed after his car collided with a military truck in Dec.,1945, and was buried with his troops at Luxembourg. His most famous quote: "The object of war is not to die for your country, but to make the other dumb bastard die for his."

Paul Road

In an area of streets named for people.

Pauline Street

Highland Gardens streets used many female names.

Paxton Road
See County Downs.

Payne Road
The current southeast city limit line.

Payson Way
Cities in Utah and Ariz.

Peabody Road
In an area with some family names for streets among other references.

Peach Street
In Oak Park and Maxwell AFB. The tree and its subacid juicy fruit are cultivated throughout the south, particularly in Chilton County, Ala.

Peachford Court
Possibly an orchard site in an area citing creeks.

Peachtree Street
Thought you had to go to Atlanta? Only to Cloverdale.

Pearl Street
Near Earl Pl. in an area of names used for streets.

Pebblebrook Drive
See Brookview Manor.

Pebble Creek Court
See Sturbridge.

■ PECAN GROVE ESTATES
Named for existing fragments of once-larger pecan groves in area. One of several developments in east Montgomery with street names taken from the rich natural environment's plantings and agriculture.

Pecan Tree Court, Drive
See Pecan Grove Estates.

Pelham Street
Central Ala. town named for John Pelham, a Confederate major who was killed in Va. in 1863.

Pelzer Avenue
W.K. Pelzer, the grandfather-in-law of developer William K. Thames, Sr.

Pembrook Court
See "Montgomery's Own Philadelphia Story."

Pendar Street

In an area of last names for streets.

Pendleton Street †

Penn Road

Possibly for William Penn, the founder of the Pennsylvania colony in 1681.

Pennsylvania Street

The state is mentioned in promotional brochure for Capitol Heights and emphasizes the connection with natural resources to establish the South as a hub for commercial and industrial growth.

Pepper Avenue

In a neighborhood of streets using last names.

Perimeter Parkway

A business area at the southeastern edge of the metropolitan area.

Perry Court, Street (N. & S.)

War of 1812 Naval Commodore Oliver Hazard Perry, who defeated the British at Lake Erie. When all thought he was doomed because of heavy gunfire to his ship, he transferred to another ship and continued the battle. He is remembered for saying, "We have met the enemy and they are ours."

Perry Hill Court, Road

This north-south road connected nearby Hill properties, to the south, with those of the Perry family, to the north.

Pershing Street

John Joseph "Black Jack" Pershing, the commander of the American Expeditionary Forces in WWI.

Persons Alley, Drive

Alley: In Cloverdale. Mrs. Alra A. Persons, the owner of the subdivision in 1914. Probably related to Gordon Persons. Dr.: Gunter Annex of Maxwell AFB; reportedly named for Gordon Persons, governor of Ala. (1951-55).

Phanton Street †

Phelan Court

In an area of streets named for people.

Phillip Street

One of five parallel streets bearing names with British connotations. May have been named for the Duke of Edinburgh,

Montgomery's Own Philadelphia Story

Large sections of Montgomery were developed in the 1950s and 1960s. While it is easy to spot "themed" neighborhoods such as the Sherwood Forest section of Forest Hills, where streets are named for characters and places in the Robin Hood legend, and the occasional family name or street named for the lay of the land, the origins of other street names are more obscure and difficult to determine, even for the people who developed the area at the time or for the children of these developers. The streets around Perry Hill and Harrison roads are especially difficult to trace since many of the area's developers are no longer active.

Everyone from Ray Amos and Billy Moore to William Thames and Donald Cameron, as well as George Cameron (Noremac Rd. is his name spelled backwards), Farm Bureau, Aronov, and York Engineering played a role in the development of the area. As Montgomery continued to grow, these developers faced a difficult imaginative task: naming over a hundred new streets in Bellehurst, Perry Hills, Forest Hills, and Lakeview Heights without duplicating other previously named streets. According to a local developer, the problem was solved when the developers began selecting street names from the Philadelphia city map. As he said, "Philly will always have more streets than Montgomery...."

or for Philip Henslowe, a theatrical manager who built the Rose Theatre (recently rediscovered and slated for reconstruction) on the south bank of the Thames River in 1595. See Kenilworth St.

Philpot Lane †

Phoebe Street †

Pickens Street

An Ala. county organized in 1820 and named for Gen. Andrew Pickens of S.C. See Chisholm.

Pickett Street

Honors either Albert J. Pickett (1810-1858), the first historian of Ala., who owned a Montgomery County plantation, Forest Farms, or C. A. Pickett, another former property owner in the area.

Pickfair Street

The name of the luxurious Hollywood home of actress Mary Pickford and her husband, Charles Fairbanks.

Piedmont Court, Drive

Probably for the Ala. town of the same name. Piedmont areas of Alabama are those lying or formed at the base of mountains, well north of Montgomery.

Pierce Street

Possibly for Franklin Pierce(1804-69), 14th president of the U.S. (1853-57), during whose administration the Young America nationalistic movement flowered. Of note: Dr. J. W. Pierce served on the city board of health in 1840.

Pierson Avenue

One of three parallel streets bearing surnames.

Pilgrim Street

Religious refugees from England, the pilgrims founded Plymouth colony in 1620 and gave New England its Puritan character. Pilgrim Missionary Baptist Church is near the intersection with Hayneville Rd.

Pill Street

A continuation of Rouse St. Honors Howard Pill, a local 1920s newspaperman and co-founder of WSFA radio.

Pine Street

The "pine" reference is frequently used in street names because of its preponderance in local forests. See Oak Park,

Maxwell AFB and Chisholm.

Pinebrook Drive, Place
Descriptive, generic.

Pine Cove
In an area of pine references. See Mosswood.

Pinecrest Drive
Situated amid other "wood" references.

Pine Forest Avenue, Drive
Both are located in areas of pine references. See also Mosswood.

Pinehaardt Drive
John H. Haardt, a local real estate developer; this street begins at intersection with Pinehill Rd.

Pinehill Road
In an area of pine references used for street names.

Pinehurst Drive
A city in N.C.

Pineleaf Street
See Highland Park.

Pineneedle Drive
Descriptive, generic.

Pine Park Drive
Located in the Dannelly Pines neighborhood.

Pine Ridge Court, Road
Situated in an area of forest references.

Pine Shadow Lane
The summer shadows of pine trees are welcome in this residential neighborhood.

Pinetop Court
See Arrowhead West.

Pinetree Lane
Located in an area of forest references.

Pine Valley Court
See Mosswood.

Pineview Street
Most forested areas in Montgomery offer pines.

Piney Curve
See Mosswood.

Pinkston Street

Green Pinkston was one of the earliest settlers in the area. He was a strong supporter of the old Antioch Baptist Church and a respected family man. He had four sons and three daughters. The youngest daughter, Evelin, married William McLemore.

Pin Oak Court

Amid Shady Oak, Burnt Hickory and other forest references.

Placid Drive

Developers' apparent wish for a peaceful neighborhood setting.

Plantation Crossing

See Sturbridge.

Plantation Ridge Road

See Sturbridge.

Plantation Way

See Pecan Grove Estates.

Planters Court, Road

See Pecan Grove Estates.

Plaza Drive

An open area in front of buildings, as at the Colony Apts. nearby. Of note: The name of one of the first motion picture theatres in the city, circa 1910.

Pleasant Avenue

Part of Philemon Sayre's tract of land.

Pleasant Ridge Road

Located in the Forest Hills community and named for the lay of the land.

Plum Street

See Oak Park.

Plummer Court, Drive

Frank Plummer, the chairman of the board of First Alabama Bank.

Plymouth Street

Near Lexington Rd., this street recalls history of Mass. colony and related events, including what most celebrate as the first Thanksgiving.

Pocahontas Road

Chief Powhatan's daughter, who, according to legend, saved

the life of Jamestown President Capt. John Smith as he was about to be beheaded by her father. She later adopted Christianity, married John Rolfe and moved to England, where she died of pneumonia in a ship awaiting favorable weather for a trans-Atlantic voyage.

Polk Street

Honors James K. Polk (1795-1849), the 11th president of the U.S. (1845-49).

Pollard Street

Possibly for Col. Charles T. Pollard, an early settler who was instrumental in the sale of bonds to build the first capitol. He was a major stockholder in the Western R.R., which ran from Montgomery to Selma, and later became president of the company. In 1835, he was elected to the board of directors of the Montgomery and Chattahoochee R.R. Co.

Ponce De Leon Avenue

The Spanish explorer Juan Ponce de Leon, who is credited with the discovery of Fla.

Poplar Street

See Oak Park and Maxwell AFB.

Portland Avenue

Honors cities in Ore. and Maine; located near another street named Augusta.

Portsmouth Drive

A city in N.H. The street is located among other New England references.

Post Oak Lane

Among streets with forest and landscape themes.

Potomac Street

For the Potomac River that begins in Md. and empties into the Chesapeake Bay.

Potts Court

See King's Hill.

Powell Avenue

T. A. Powell, the surveyor for the Highland Gardens area in the 1920s.

Powelldale Drive

Frank Powell, the owner of Powell Electric Co. The neighborhood bears this name.

Prairie Lane
See Halcyon.

Prairie Creek Trail
Descriptive of the landscape near Baldwin Slough.

Prairie Vista
Surrounded by references to meadows.

Pratt Court
Located on Gunter Annex of Maxwell AFB, the street was probably named in memory of Pvt. Clyde Pratt, killed in an air crash in 1921.

Preakness Path
The Preakness, begun in 1873, is run at Pimlico Racetrack in Baltimore. In a neighborhood of streets with names taken from horse racing. See Taylor Crossing.

Presidents Drive
Situated in Executive Park.

Preston Place †

Price Street
Harold Price, the executive vice president of Southern United Life Insurance Co.

Primrose Lane
Primrose is the common name for at least 400 species of herbs.

Prince Street †

Prince George Drive
George III, King of England and Ireland during the American Revolution. Since he shared the blame for the loss of the colonies, he was very unpopular with his subjects during the 1770s. He suffered a recurrence of mental illness and died at Windsor—insane and blind—in 1820.

Princess Ann Court, Street
In an area with English names and references. Probably for Princess Anne, daughter of Elizabeth II and Prince Philip of Great Britain.

Princeton Road
Honors Princeton University located in Princeton, N.J.

Proctor Street †

Provost Avenue
The maiden name of the ex-wife of Frank Garrett, the devel-

oper of this area.

Pugh Street

For James Lawrence Pugh (1819-1907), who served in the Confederate Congress and in the U.S. Senate (1880-97). He refused a position on the U.S. Supreme Court in 1888 because of his age.

Putnam Street

Possibly related to settlement in Marengo County named for a local family reputedly related to Revolutionary War Gen. Israel Putnam (1718-1790).

Q

Quail Ridge Drive

Amid streets with names of rural, forest and landscape features.

Quebec Street

A city on the St. Lawrence River founded in 1608. The largest province in Canada.

Queen Elizabeth Court

The monarch of England for much of Shakespeare's life. Elizabeth II ruled England when this area was developed. See Wynton M. Blount Cultural Park.

Queensbury Court, Drive

The title of Sir John Sholto Douglas, a British aristocrat and boxing promoter, who formulated the Marquis of Queensbury rules to govern boxing. In a neighborhood of several streets with English references.

Queens Hollow Court

Amid English references for streets.

Quenby Court, Drive †

Quercus Street

Genus name for a variety of oak that grows in wetlands.

Quincy Court

Possibly for the city in Mass. that was the home of the John and John Quincy Adams family.

R

Rabbit Road

Probably named for rural feature of the area.

Race Street

Reputed to be the former site of a horse racing track. The sport was popular and accepted in the city until the mid-1930s.

Radburn Road

An experimental city in N.J. designed in 1927 to protect residents from air pollution, noise and other problems of congested city life.

Radcliffe Road

A college named for colonist Ann Radcliffe, who in 1638 contributed funds for establishment of Harvard University. Radcliffe College, opened in 1894, is now affiliated with Harvard.

Raffles Drive

Chosen by Paul Corwin because it is unusual. Of interest: A gentleman burglar in turn-of-the-century novels.

Railroad Street

Crosses the Louisville and Nashville R.R.

Railway Street

Perpendicular to the Seaboard R.R., which runs through this subdivision.

Rainbow Curve, Road

The rainbow is an enduring symbol of joy. In the Bible, God sent a rainbow to assure Noah that the world would never again be flooded. The street is located in Sunshine Acres.

Raintree Drive

Raintree County, popular novel and film romance about the time this area was developed. The book was written by Ross Lockridge, Jr., and published in 1948. The 1957 film starred Elizabeth Taylor and Montgomery Clift.

Ramos Court

See Forest Hills.

Ramp Road

Located on Gunter Annex of Maxwell AFB, originally an airplane ramp leading to one of the hangars. The old ramp was put into use as a street when Gunter's mission no longer required the use of aircraft. One of the hangars now houses the commissary.

Ramsey Road

In an area with people's last names used for streets.

Ranch Drive

An area once owned by the Bowman family; site of pecan orchards.

Randolph Street

John Randolph, a statesman and member of the First Continental Congress. Also, on Maxwell AFB, memorializing Capt. William Millican Randolph, whose military career began in 1916 on the Mexican border. He served in WWI, was appointed CO of the 25th Bomb Squadron at France Field in Panama 1924-27 and served as adjutant of the Air Corps Advance Flying School. He and his sons all died in aircraft accidents.

Rane Drive

In a neighborhood using names for streets. Of interest: "Rane" is a corruption of "rani," meaning reigning Hindu queen.

Ranier Ridge

The developer, William Nicrosi, once lived in Seattle, Wash., near Mt. Ranier.

Ravenwood Drive

In an area with "wood" in many street names.

Ray Drive

In a neighborhood using people's names for streets.

Rebekah Lane

In a neighborhood using people's names for streets.

Red Barn Road

See Carriage Hills.

Redbud Drive

An ornamental tree that is favored by the area's landscapers.

Red Oak Court

In an area with street names of the countryside.

Reese Ferry Road

A prominent pioneer family that settled across the river in Autauga County. Of interest: Perry Reese was a member of the 1st regiment Texas volunteers, a group formed in the city and dispatched to Texas to aid in the fight for independence from Mexico. All of his company were killed after they surrendered in March 1836.

Regal Drive

Near Queensbury Dr., another street with English associations.

■ REGENCY PARK

Developed by William Thames, these streets have diverse themes ranging from family names to English cities and elements of nature.

Regent Drive

One who rules in place of the monarch.

Reid Street

Located on lands owned by the Reid family in 1903. J. W. T. Reid was both auctioneer and grocer during the 1830s.

Rembert Street

Possibly for the family of James Monroe Rembert, a planter and the owner of Rembert Hills Plantation in Marengo County.

Remington Court, Road

In 1850, a Mr. Remington claimed that he had discovered a new principle in bridge building. He constructed a single-span bridge over 400 feet long over a ravine at the foot of Coosa St.

Renee Drive

In an area of women's first names used for streets.

Reston Place

Urban community, an original concept in urban planning in Fairfax County, Va.

Retreat Road

A place to which to escape.

Reuben Street

See Capitol Heights.

Rex Street

Honors Rex Turner, the former president of Alabama Christian College.

Rexford Court, Road

See Georgetown.

Rhodes Street

For Joseph Lee Rhodes, president of W. Virginia Land Co., the developers of the Uplands subdivision near Highland Park in 1906. Uplands included Spruce, Teague, Bryan, and Owens streets.

Rialto Drive

Probably named for the old Rialto Hotel, built in 1836 by Lewis W. Pond.

Rice Street

Samuel Farrow Rice, a former Ala. Supreme Court chief justice (1856-59).

Rich Road

In a neighborhood using people's last names for streets.

Richard Road

Richard Gordon, grandson of Geraldine LeCroy, developer of the LeCroy Shopping Center.

Richmond Court, Road

Montgomery was the first Confederate capital; Richmond, Va., was the second. In an area of city names used for streets.

Rick Drive (N. & S.)

In an area of people's names used for streets.

Riderwood Drive

In an area that once offered forest paths for riders.

Ridge Avenue, Street

At the ridge adjacent to Cramton Bowl. Built on a natural rise as part of the Cloverdale Garden suburb. See Cloverdale.

Ridgecrest Street

In the Ridgecrest neighborhood.

Ridgefield Drive

In the Ridgefield neighborhood.

Ridgemont Avenue, Court

Located in the Ridgecrest neighborhood, at what was once the southern ridge of Montgomery.

Ridge Park Court, Road

Adjoins high land in east Montgomery that bears the Auburn University at Montgomery water tower.

Ridgeway (E. & W.)

Descriptive, generic.

Ridgewood Lane

For the lay of the land in Forest Hills.

Rigby Street

See Highland Gardens.

Riley Road

In an area with many family names for streets.

Ripley Street (N. & S.)

Honors Gen. Eleazar Ripley, who fought at the Battle of Niagara during the War of 1812.

Rita Lane

In an area including other given names, such as Laverne.

River Road

Follows the bank of the Alabama River on Maxwell AFB.

Riverside Drive

A short street near Maxwell AFB that terminates at the Alabama River near the Confederate powder magazine.

Riverview Street

Two streets at separate bends of the Alabama River in the northern downtown area.

Riviera Road

A narrow coastal region between the Alps and the Mediterranean Sea extending from southeast France to northwest Italy, a popular resort area.

Roanoke Street

Town in Ala.,Va., N.C., Ill., Ind. and La.; a river in Va. and N. C.; an island off the coast of N. Carolina, the site of Raleigh's unsuccessful colonizing attempts (1585-87).

Robbins Road

See Forest Hills.

Robert C. Hatch Drive

A longtime professor at Alabama State University and consultant on African-American education in Ala.

Robison Hill Road

Landowners Laura C. Robison and her son, Vaughn Hill, a Montgomery attorney. The name of the street is incorrectly used as "Robinson Hill" on some maps, street signs and businesses.

Robinson Street

Honors James Jefferson Robinson (1840-1919), a state senator in the late 1880s who served as a member of the 1901 Ala. Constitutional Convention.

Rock Rose Court
In a neighborhood with botanical street names.

Rogers Street
For Charlie Rogers, the first manager of the Montgomery Housing Authority and the son-in-law of Mayor William A. Gunter.

Rojon Court
Appears to be a combination of two names.

Rolind Drive
In an area of men's and women's names used for streets.

Rolling Road, Rolling Road Circle
For the features of the terrain.

Roosevelt Street
Theodore "Teddy" Roosevelt (1858-1919), the 26th president of the U.S. (1901-09).

Rosalie Drive
See Wynlakes.

Rosa L. Parks Avenue
Prev. Plank Rd., for planking used originally to pave the street (copying a Russian method that did not work in the South because the wood rotted so quickly); changed in 1880s to Cleveland Ave. honoring Grover Cleveland, the first Democratic president after the Civil War to visit Montgomery. In 1986 the City Council voted unanimously to change the name to Rosa Parks Ave. for the catalyst of the 1955 Montgomery Bus Boycott that gave impetus to the Civil Rights movement.

Rose Lane
Rose Cramton, the wife of Highland Gardens' developer Fred J. Cramton. See Highland Gardens and Cramton Bowl.

Rosebud Court
In an area of tree names used for streets.

Rosedale Drive
Suggesting gardens, and located near Biltmore Ave.

Rosedon Court, Drive
In an area of family names used for streets.

Rosemary Road (W.)
Of interest: a fragrant shrub of the mint family that is used in

perfumes and as a seasoning. In a neighborhood of names of people used for streets.

Rosemont Circle, Court, Drive, Place, Terrace

For Rosemont Gardens, a major floral enterprise founded by the Paterson family.

Rosewood Drive

A popular name for a group of tropical woods known for their beauty and use in making fine furniture.

Roslyn Drive

In an area of people's names used for streets.

Ross Street

Named as part of the Jno. W. Watts plat in 1884.

Roswell Place †

Rotary Street

An organization of business and professional men, founded in 1905 and in Montgomery in 1917, to promote helpfulness and thoughtfulness in business life.

Roundtree Road

Descriptive, generic.

Rouse Street

Honors L. D. Rouse, a Montgomery land developer. Continues as Pill St. for Howard Pill. Rouse was a prominent business leader; Pill was a newspaper man and co-founder of WSFA radio during the 1920s. See Pill St.

Rouse Ridge Court, Road

For L.D. Rouse, a Montgomery land developer.

Roxana Court, Road

See "Montgomery's Own Philadelphia Story."

Roxboro Drive

In an area of place references used for streets.

Royal Carriage Drive

See Carriage Hills.

Royal Creek Road

Near Cross Creek.

Royal Crest Court, Drive, Mews

In keeping with the British royalty motif. Probably the royal crest or coat-of-arms of Great Britain's royal family. "Mews" means an alley behind houses for stables or barns.

Royal Downing Court

For Downing St., Westminster, London; the location of the official residences of the prime minister and the chancellor of the exchequer.

Royal Oak Court

See Halcyon.

Royal Park Street

Descriptive, generic.

Runnymede Drive

A meadow in England believed to be where the Magna Carta was signed in 1215. See Taylor Crossing.

Rush Drive

One of a group of last names used for streets in this area.

Rushing Street

W. B. Rushing, the owner of the property.

Rushton Ridge †

Russell Street

For the Ala. county organized in 1832 and named for Col. Gilbert C. Russell, a Creek War veteran.

Rutgers Loop (E. & W.)

Honors the state university of N. J., founded in 1766 and located in New Brunswick. See College Grove.

Ruth Avenue

Possibly for the family of Charles Leon Ruth II, a former prominent Montgomery optometrist and grandson of Charles Leonidas Ruth, who was a Montgomery alderman in 1899.

Rutland Street

Local developer James Rutland.

Ryan Street

Honors William John Ryan, the mayor of Capitol Heights during WWI and promoter of the area for residential development.

S

Saccapatoy Drive

A small effluent of Hatchet Creek in Coosa County; village of Saccapatoy Creek in the same county; Sakapatayi, an Upper Creek town situated on creek of same name; possibly derivative of Creek "Sakapotogas," for "I lie inside," the term referring to water lilies, the seeds of which were eaten by the natives.

Saddlewood Lane

Among a group of streets with "wood" as part of names: Blythewood, Hollow Wood, Charing Wood; located near Forest Ridge.

Sadler Street

Prev. Railroad St., now honors Joe Sadler, who for 20 years was the superintendent of carrier and parcel post delivery for the U.S. Postal Service and was responsible, after passage of a 1951 city ordinance, for changing street names and numbers to eliminate duplications which were "a headache," he said. Noting in the late 1950s that Montgomery was growing quickly, Sadler opted for a career change. As a contractor, he designed and built more than 1,600 residences. In addition, he planned the street layouts for several subdivisions.

Sagamore Drive

Algonquin for a subordinate chief; Sagamore Hill was Theodore Roosevelt's New York home, completed in 1885.

Sagewood Court, Drive

Botanical and rural references in this area.

Saleary Road

In an area of people's names used for streets.

Salem Drive

One of three parallel streets named for cigarette brands; also, Salem, N.C.

Salinas Court

A city in Calif.; located in an area of streets named for cities.

Salisbury Place

For John Montague, the Earl of Salisbury; a historical figure and minor character in Shakespeare's *Richard III*. See "Wynton M. Blount Cultural Park."

Samantha Drive

In an area using several women's first names for streets.

Samar Drive

The first archipelago to be discovered by Spaniards (1521), in present-day Philippines in the Samar Sea. The area was incorporated into the city in 1949, after WWII, which may account for the reference to the Philippines.

Samaritan Road
In the gospel of Luke, the Samaritan was a despised outsider and yet the only one to stop and help an injured traveler.

Sampson Street
In an area of people's names used for streets.

Sanders Lane
See Dagger Hole Rd.

Sandfield Trail
See Arrowhead West.

Sandhill
See Wynlakes.

Sandhurst Drive
A town in England, the site of the Royal Military Academy. In an area with some English references.

Sandra Street
In an area of first names used for streets.

Sandstone Court
A porous rock formed of grains of sand cemented together by clay or silica. In an area with rock types used for street names.

Sandy Street
In a group of people's names used for streets.

Sandy Bluff Court
An area of street names for topographical features.

Sandy Ridge Curve, Lane
Descriptive, generic.

Sanford Street
Possibly for J. W. A. Sanford, the attorney general in the 1870s. Listed on the Reid plat in 1903.

Sansone Court, Road †

Santee Drive
An eastern branch of the Sioux.

Saratoga Lane
Developer William Nicrosi's Crommelin ancestors moved from Saratoga, N.Y., to Wetumpka, where they built an inn near a spring hoping to recreate the atmosphere of their former residence.

Sarita Court
A town in Texas.

Sarver Avenue
In an area of first and last names used for streets.

Savage Drive
Possibly for Monseignor Dennis Savage, a former priest at St. Peter's Catholic Church around the turn of the century.

Savannah Drive
Tropical or subtropical grassland containing scattered trees or bushes characteristic of tropical America and much of tropical Africa. A city in Ga. that was captured by Union Gen. Sherman during the Civil War. Interesting note: Savannah Jack was a notorious figure who led a band of hostile Indians in this area around 1818.

Savoy Street
Range of Alps in southeast France. Famed hotel in London.

Sawston Court
In an area of English-themed references.

Sawyer Lane
One who cuts wood; this street is situated amid other forest references. Of interest: The Rev. Seymour B. Sawyer was pastor of the Methodist church in the city during the 1830s.

Saxon Court
See Halcyon.

Sayre Street
William and Daniel Sayre arrived in Montgomery in 1819. William was one of the founders of the First Presbyterian Church and built what became the First White House of the Confederacy. Daniel was the editor of the *Montgomery Post* and father of Justice Anthony Sayre, who served in both houses of the Ala. Legislature and was an associate judge of the Ala. Supreme Ct. Anthony Sayre was the father of Zelda Sayre Fitzgerald. This was the first Montgomery street to be paved with asphalt, in 1902.

Schley Street
For Winfield Scott Schley, an American naval commander during the Spanish-American War.

Scott Street
Honors Gen. John Scott, who purchased the land adjacent to

Andrew Dexter's and founded "East Alabama." See "Why Downtown StreetsDon't Meet: The Street Conflict."

Seaboard Street

Parallels the Seaboard R.R., which runs through this subdivision.

Seaton Boulevard, Place

See Sturbridge.

Seay Street

Honors Thomas Seay (1846-1896), an Ala. senator (1867-77) and the state's 23rd governor (1884).

Sedgefield Lane

Sedge is a grasslike herb; its hardiest varieties can be woven into baskets.

Seeger Street

In an area of last names used for streets.

Selfridge Street

On Maxwell AFB, memorializing 1st Lt. Thomas Etholen Selfridge, the first army officer to fly a powered airplane and the first military casualty of powered flight. He flew with Orville Wright at Fort Meyer, Va., in 1908. His plane crashed, putting Wright in the hospital for several months and killing Selfridge.

Seibles Road

Col. John Jacobs Seibles raised a battalion of men from the area during the Mexican War. They were stationed at Orizaga. In 1849 he became the editor of the *Montgomery Advertiser*. When Wilson's Raiders came on April 12, 1865, Seibles was instrumental in persuading Gen. Wilson to maintain control of his troops and avoid widespread destruction of private property. Later, during the 1930s, Fannie Marks Seibles co-founded the city's first Museum of Fine Arts in the old Central High School building on the corner of Lawrence and High streets.

Selma Highway

The main route from Montgomery west to Selma.

Selman Street †

Semaht Drive

Name of developer William K. Thames, Sr., spelled backwards. His name is spelled forwards on a nearby street.

Seminole Circle, Court, Drive, Place

A tribe of the Muskhogean family, allied to the Hitchiti and Creek who lived in southern Ga. and northern Fla.

Semmes Drive

Pobably for Raphael Semmes, the commander of the Confederate raider *Alabama*. He is best known for running Federal blockades, harrassing the Union navy, and his battle with the Union man-of-war *Kearsarge*, in which he managed to escape to England. After the war, the U.S. Navy Department tried and failed to convict the admiral for treason.

Semple Street

For H. C. Semple, the owner and developer of nearby property in the late 1800s.

Senators Drive

An Auburn University at Montgomery street that honors the school mascot.

Senderson Court †

Sequoia Drive

In a neighborhood with botanical street names, especially trees. Also see Maxwell AFB.

Seth Johnson Drive

Seth Johnson's father moved the family here in the 1800s after he traded a family hotel in Red Oak, Iowa, for large acreages in this area. Seth Johnson, cattle rancher and farmer, was active in community affairs, sponsoring the Red Cross drive for several years and serving as a charter member of the Alabama Farm Bureau. His land holdings stretched from what is now Carol Villa to the Seth Johnson School area. He had 12 children who inherited his lands. Charles McIntyre Johnson sold the Carol Villa area to developers, but some streets there still bear Johnson family names.

Shadeland Drive

Woods and shade are popular images for suburban street names. In an area of streets with rural names.

Shades Valley Drive (E. & W.)

Descriptive, generic.

Shadow Lane

A shady, wooded street.

Shadowood Court Road

In an area with botanical street names, especially trees.

Shady Street

Probably once a tree-lined street. Located near the Alabama River.

Shady Grove Drive

See Pecan Grove Estates.

Shady Oak Lane

In an area of streets named for woods and creeks.

Shadyside Lane

Located in a neighborhood with a "wood" theme.

Shaffer Ridge Court

See Wyndridge.

Shafter Street

In a series of parallel streets with family names.

Shagg Street

In a neighborhood of streets with family names.

Shamrock Court, Lane

A variety of clover; the symbol of Ireland and a traditional symbol of good luck.

Shannon Hill Road †

Sharkey Street

Possibly William Lewis Sharkey, a former governor of Miss., and also a former U. S. Senator.

Sharon Court, Lane

In a neighborhood of streets using women's first names.

Sharp Street

Named as part of the Jno. W. Watts plat in 1884.

Shawnee Drive (E. & W.)

Developed by Shawnee Terrace Inc.

Sheffield Court, Road

Possibly for James Lawrence Sheffied (1819-1892), a Civil War hero and state senator who was instrumental in the construction of the Confederate Monument in Montgomery.

Sheldon Lane

Honors Sheldon Martin.

Shelly Court, Lane

See Chisholm.

Shenandoah Drive

Historic Shenandoah Valley in Va.; located in an area with

several references to places and events in that state.

Shep Court †

Shepard Street
In an area of last names used for streets.

Sherburn Road
See Regency Park.

Sheridan Alley, Court, Street
Three alleys come off Sheridan St., off Mobile Rd. and near Lincoln St., a possible connection of Civil War leaders. Ct.: In Camp Sheridan, created for WWI mobilization. Camp Sheridan was probably named for Union Gen. Philip Sheridan. It was established by the federal government near Montgomery in 1917, the same time that Camp McClellan was organized near Anniston. Both were used as infantry training and mobilization sites. See Vandiver Blvd., Ct., St.

Sherman Way
See "Montgomery's Own Philadelphia Story."

Sherwood Drive
Forest in Robin Hood legend. See Forest Hills.

Shirley Lane
A Carol Villa street that was probably named by newer developers than the Johnson family, the original landowners.

Shoreham Drive
A city in N.Y. and also a noted hotel in Washington, D.C.

Short Street
One of the shortest streets in the city.

Short Line Circle, Drive
Short Line R.R. See Bell Station.

Shreve Street
For J.H. Shreve, the subdivision owner in 1906.

Shumacher Avenue E.
Prev. Avenue B, on Maxwell AFB, redesignated to memorialize Lt. Charles H. Shumacher, who was the first person to be killed in an airplane crash at Maxwell Field. He died in 1919.

Sierra Street
A Spanish word meaning "a chain of hills or mountains," the peaks of which suggest the teeth of a saw.

Silver Lane

Located near the area where Laura S. Croom Hill buried her silver when James Harrison Wilson and his raiders rode through Montgomery on April 12, 1865, on his way through Ga. and Ala. While in Montgomery, he made the Teague House at 440 S. Perry St. his headquarters.

Simmons Drive †

Simpson Street

Probably for Hugh or S. M. Simpson, the area landowners in 1907.

Singleton Street

Developed by Frank Garrett and named for a former college roommate.

Sir Michael Drive

See Forest Hills.

Sixth Street

One of three streets in a series including only Sixth, Eighth and Ninth streets.

Skyline Avenue

This street is on the ridge of an extension of King's Hill.

Slauson Circle (N. & S.)

For Ben, Gary, Clayburn and other members of the Slauson family. Lonnie Slauson, a clerk at a downtown drugstore at the corner of Bibb and Commerce streets, eventually bought the business and named it Lonnie's Sundries.

Smallbrook Drive

Descriptive of the area before its development; very close to Baldwin Slough.

Smiley Circle (N., S., E. & W.)

The Rev. George Washington Smiley, a local community and church leader, who served as the first and only moderator of the Galilee District Association and served his church for 61 years.

Smith Street

Smith streets in Maxwell Heights, Jackson Ferry Pk. Possibly for family of William Henry Smith (1814-90), a Montgomery planter and cotton merchant, or another William Smith, Ala. governor 1868-70. See Jackson Ferry Pk.

Smythe Curve, Street

Honors W. D. Smythe, who developed the property in the 1870s.

Sneed Road

Located on Gunter Annex of Maxwell AFB, the street probably honors Maj. Albert L. Sneed, who particpated in a transcontinental aerial contest in 1919. Planned by Billy Mitchell, the contest was designed to test both personnel and equipment. He flew a DH-4 through fog and snow and was forced to make an emergency landing in Buffalo, N.Y. The plane bounced and crashed into the ground nose-first; his flying partner was killed, but Maj. Sneed survived.

Sommerville Court, Drive

For Robert Sommerville Hill, one of the sons of Laura S. and Luther Leonidas Hill.

Sonnie Court †

South Boulevard, Drive, Street

Blvd.: Also called Southern Bypass, part of the perimeter route originally intended to bypass the city. Dr.: on Gunter Annex of Maxwell AFB, running roughly east to west along southern boundary on the eastern side of the base; St.: once the southern boundary of the city.

Southdale Drive

Situated in south Montgomery.

South Hampton Drive

In an area of English-themed references, for Hampton Court or for the city of Southampton.

Southlawn Court, Drive

Located in the Southlawn neighborhood.

Southmont Court, Drive

Both marked the southern boundary of Montgomery at the time they were named.

Southview Avenue

Part of the Thomas estate, located on the far south side of Montgomery at the time it was developed.

Southwest Street

In southwest Montgomery.

Southwood Drive

Off South Blvd.

Spaatz Street

Prev. 2nd St. on Gunter Annex of Maxwell AFB, renamed to honor Sgt. Harold Spaatz who, was one of the first U.S. airmen to be executed by the Japanese military after a mock trial for the Doolittle Raid. Although protected by the Geneva Convention, he was beheaded in 1942 for alleged war crimes against Japan.

Spann Place

Charles S. Spann, owner of the property.

Spaulding Drive

In a neighborhood of last names used for streets.

Speigle Street

See Highland Gardens.

Spenseth Drive

Spencer and Seth Johnson, two of the 12 children of rancher and farmer Seth Johnson. See Seth Johnson Dr.

Spivey Court

Betty Spivey, the secretary to Volz and Leon Capouano, a firm of two Montgomery attorneys; they were also investors in Brighton Estates.

Springfield Drive

Cities in Ill., Mass. and Mo.

Springhill Avenue

Possibly for Spring Hill College in Mobile.

Spring Park Court, Drive

Located in the Spring Park neighborhood.

Spring Valley Road

In Spring Valley neighborhood.

Spruce Curve, Street

See Oak Park and Maxwell AFB.

St. Charles Avenue

See Capitol Heights.

St. Clair

An Ala. county organized in 1818 and named for Gen. Arthur St. Clair of Penn.

St. James Street

One St. James was the brother of Jesus; another was the brother of St. John.

St. John Street

One of the 12 apostles, traditional author of the fourth gospel.

St. Louis Street

The largest city in Mo., it was the site of the international exposition in 1904 commemorating the centennial of the Louisiana Purchase.

St. Lukes Drive

One of the 12 apostles, thought to be the author of the third gospel.

Stable Gate Court

In an area with horse racing themes used for streets.

Stakely Drive

Dr. Charles Stakely, the pastor of the First Baptist Church from 1902 until his retirement in 1930.

Stallings Drive

Dan Stallings, a local realtor.

Stamford Court

Cities in England and Conn.

Stanford Avenue †

Located on Gunter Annex of Maxwell AFB.

Stanley Drive, Street

Dr.: In an area of last names used for streets. St.: Possibly a former landowner or for Cash Stanley, the former editor of the *Alabama Journal*.

Starbrook Drive

See Brookview Manor.

Starr Alley, Street

Listed as part of the Pebworth property in 1889. Possibly for the family of Lucius Ernest Starr (1838-1913), a Montgomery doctor and Civil War hero.

State Street

The state of Ala.

Station Court

See Bell Station.

Steeplechase Lane

See Carriage Hills.

Stella Street

Named by W. D. Westcott in 1906.

Stephens Street

Named as part of W. D. Westcott's estate, Woodrow Place, in 1912, possibly for J. B. Stephens, a nearby landowner.

Sterling Drive

See "Montgomery's Own Philadelphia Story."

Stillbrook Lane

Located amid other outdoor references used for streets in a neighborhood with a park and lakes.

Still Oaks Drive

Amid other outdoor references used for streets in a neighborhood with a park and lakes.

Stokes Road, Street

Rd.: Probably for the former landowner. St.: Andrew Jackson Stokes, the pastor of Columbus St. Baptist Church, which later became First Baptist Church.

Stone Street

An early Montgomery family. George W. Stone was an associate justice of the Ala. Supreme Court in the 1870s.

Stonecliff Court

Pleasant-sounding, generic.

Stonewood Court, Drive

Pleasant-sounding, generic.

Stovall Lane †

Stowers Place

For real estate developer John Walter Stowers, Sr.

Straightaway Drive

See County Downs.

Stratford Drive, Lane

Dr.: For a prominent landowning family in the late 1800s. J. C. Stratford was a bookkeeper for the 1st National Bank in 1878; La.: For Stratford, England, Shakespeare's birthplace.

Strathmore Drive

The Earl of Strathmore is a hereditary title in England.

Stratton Court

A town in England located southwest of Barnstaple near the Atlantic coast. Also of interest: Charles Stratton was the real name of Tom Thumb.

Stribling Street
2nd Lt. W. L. Stribling came to Maxwell AFB in 1930. He was a strong contender for the heavyweight boxing title. See Dempsey St.

Strickland Court
Located on Gunter Annex of Maxwell AFB, the street probably honors Capt. Auby C. Strickland, who flew a refueling plane used to keep the *Question Mark* in the air for more than 150 hours. The *Question Mark*, commanded by Maj. Carl Spatz, took off from Los Angeles on New Year's Day, 1929, and stayed aloft for a week despite fog and rough weather.

Stroll Drive
In an area of last names used for streets.

Stuart Street
For a Montgomery construction executive Mose Stuart.

■ STURBRIDGE
These names were chosen to reflect a Southern country flavor.

Sturbridge Drive, Place
A neighborhood that was developed on the site of the former Wible farm.

Sudie Street
One of a series of streets named for females in the Bel Air development owned by A.G. Tuttle in the 1880s.

Sultan Court
The Delhi Sultanate was the first Muslim empire of India. It was destroyed by Hindu forces in 1398.

Sumerset Lane
See Forest Hills.

Summerhill Court, Drive, Ridge
See McGehee Pl.

Summitt Street
See Highland Park.

Sumter Avenue
A city in S.C. and also the name of the fort in Charleston harbor where the first shot of the War Between the States was fired. The telegram bearing the order to "reduce the fort as

your judgement decides to be most practical" was sent from the Winter Building, which still stands near the fountain on Dexter Ave. Also, for Sumter County, organized in 1832 and named for Gen. Thomas Sumter of S.C.

Sunnybrook Drive

Rebecca of Sunnybrook Farm, a popular novel by Kate Douglas Wiggin published in 1903.

Sunset Drive, Street

Dr.: Located on a hill and named for its view. St.: Suggestive of the pleasant country atmosphere promised in the Highland Gardens subdivision.

Sunshine Drive

Located in the Sunshine Acres neighborhood.

Surrey Road

A Carol Villa street that was probably named by newer developers than the Seth Johnson family, original landowners.

Susan Drive

In an area with women's first names used for several streets.

Sussex Drive

For an Anglo-Saxon kingdom, the southernmost county of England. The street is also one of Montgomery's southernmost streets and is located in an area of English references.

Sutherland Drive (N. & S.)

Situated in an area of English place name references.

Sutter Street

William Sutter and his brother owned a grocery store in the city in the 1870s.

Sutton Drive

Cities in Mass. and Texas. Also a long-time area family name.

Suwanee Drive

A city in Ga., home of the Atlanta Falcons, and also a Fla. river.

Swan Street

A regal bird gracing area lakes. Located near streets bearing bird names.

Sweetbriar Road

A Eurasian flower with pink and red flowers. A college in Va. Located in an area with garden references for streets.

Sweeten Creek Road
Situated near a watercourse.

Sweet Gum Drive
In a neighborhood with botanical street names, especially trees.

Sweet Meadow Drive
Among other streets with "sweet" and "meadow" in their names.

Sweetwood Way
Among other streets with "sweet" and "wood" references.

Sycamore Court, Drive, Street
Ct., Dr.: In a neighborhood with botanical street names, especially trees. St: Also, see Maxwell AFB.

Sylvan Drive
Descriptive term derived from the Latin "sylva" (forest).

Sylvest Drive
For Burke Sylvest, who once owned this property.

T

Taft Street
Possibly for William Howard Taft (1857-1930), the 27th U.S. president of U.S. (1909-13), and chief justice of the Supreme Court (1921-30).

Talbot Terrace
Honors Talbot Griffin, an area realtor.

Tallapoosa Street
An Ala. county and river. The name comes from an Upper Creek Indian town whose Choctaw name "talipushi" means "pulverized rock."

Tall Timber Court
Situated near other streets with outdoor references.

Talon Court
The claw of a bird of prey.

Tandy Drive †

Tanglewood Drive
The music festival in Mass.; also, the name of a group of children's stories by Nathanial Hawthorne.

Tankersley Road

For Corrie Hill Tankersley and her sons: Dr. Felix Tankersley, a Montgomery obstetrician, and Will Hill Tankersley, an investment banker.

Tankview Court

The location of Russell Petroleum Corp.

Tara Lane

For the Tara Plantation in *Gone With the Wind*, by Margaret Mitchell.

Tatum Street

Honors M. T. Tatum, the Montgomery intendant (mayor) in the 1830s.

Taylor Circle, Road (N.), Street

Cir, Rd.: Possibly for Dr. Thomas Burge Taylor, the owner of Chantilly Plantation, which was later inherited by his nephew, the owner of Taylor's Store at Waugh, and related to the McLemore family, area landowners. St.: See King's Hill.

■ TAYLOR CROSSING

A horse-racing theme is used in naming the streets in this neighborhood.

Taylor Park Road

See Taylor Circle.

Teague Street

Named as part of The Uplands subdivision by Joseph Lee Rhodes of the West Virginia Land Co. in 1906. Possibly for Robert Sterling Teague or his son William Martin Teague, founders of Teague and Sons Hardware in 1875. By 1975, sales had topped $8 million. The family sold the firm in 1978.

Teal Drive

A variety of freshwater duck.

Technacenter Drive

The location of Technacenter Research Park, affiliated with Auburn University and Auburn University at Montgomery.

Tecumseh Drive

Celebrated Shawnee chief who sought to create a great Indian state by uniting various tribes.

Telsie Road

Among other last names used for streets.

Tensaw Lane

A settlement of Ta-en-sau Indians that bordered on the Mobile and Alabama rivers.

Teresa Street

A member of the Miller family, who were close friends of Highland Gardens' developer, Fred Cramton. See Cramton Bowl and Highland Gardens.

Teri Court

For Teri Aronov Grusin, the daughter of Aaron Aronov, a local realtor.

Terminal Road

Runs west from Mobile Rd. to Montgomery Industrial Terminal.

Terrace Avenue

Lined by streets with terraced yards.

Terrace Cove

See Wyndridge.

Texas Court, Street

For the state of Texas; intersected by Austin St.

Thach Road

A major road in Auburn that runs by the university's Samford Hall.

Thames Court, Lane

For William K. Thames, Sr., a local developer. It is parallel to Semaht St., which is Thames spelled backwards.

Thistlewood Court

See Halcyon.

Thomas Avenue, Court

Ave.: For Jett M. Thomas' family plantation home "Edgewood," built in 1821 and located on present-day Thomas Avenue. Ct.: In a group of streets bearing people's names.

Thomason Avenue

Honors M. R. Thomason, a local road building contractor.

Thorington Road

A prominent early Montgomery family from Ireland. A former Ala. State Bar Association President (1909), William Sewell Thorington, who also served as an associate justice of the Ala. Supreme Court in 1912. Also of note: Jack Thorington was the president of the Montgomery and Wetumpka Plank Rd.

Co., established Jan. 18, 1850. (See Rosa L. Parks Ave.) He served as mayor (1839-44) and achieved the rank of colonel during the Civil War. He died in 1871 and is buried at Oakwood Cemetery.

Thorn Place

Thorn bushes along this street in the early 20th century are said to have inspired the name. See Cloverdale.

Thornhill Drive

A Carol Villa street probably named by newer developers than the Johnson family, original landowners.

Thornton Road

Honors Bill Thornton, a local developer and grocer.

Thornwood Drive

Located among other references to woods and trees in street names.

Thousand Oaks Drive

Descriptive of a former oak grove or a reference to the Calif. community.

Thrasher Street

Allie L. Thrasher, former owner of the property. One of a series of streets in the Lee High School area named by 1920s developers for women's names, natural features and family names.

Timberline Road

Located in hilly, tree-filled Mountainview Estates.

Timbermill Court, Drive

See Wynlakes.

Tine Avenue

Honors Tine Davis, late Winn-Dixie executive and philanthropist.

Tioga Road

For cities in N.Y. and Penn.

Todd Road

The George H. Todd family owned approximately 15 acres here during the first half of the 1900s, and raised bamboo cane for fishing poles with root stock imported from Japan. The family still retains correspondence relating to the purchase of the roots. See George Todd Dr.

Toledo Court

A city in Spain infamous as the seat of the Spanish Inquisition. See Monterey Park.

Tolvert Street

See Highland Gardens.

Towne Lake Court, Drive, Place

The developer wanted a name to suggest a closeness to the city while retaining a rural atmosphere. Name of subdivision.

Townsend Drive

Of note: the Townsend Acts were initial taxation statues that irritated the American colonists and eventually led to rebellion. In an area of English-themed references. Also of interest: Mrs. A. Townsend, a teacher, and G. W. Townsend, a lawyer, are listed in M. P. Blue's 1878 *City Directory*.

Traction Avenue

Prev. Hannah St. Changed to Traction Ave. because it paralleled the Montgomery Traction Car Line, one of the early streetcar lines in the city.

Trade Center Street

Located downtown among a number of streets developed before 1900, this street was probably a center of trade.

Travis Street

Possibly named for William Travis, a hero of the Alamo, or for a local family.

Tremont Street

Possibly for the Boston street that is home to three famous hotels.

Trinity Boulevard (E.), Road

Blvd.: Location of the Trinity Presbyterian School; Rd.: The site of Trinity Baptist Church.

Triple Crown Drive

See County Downs.

Trotting Path

See Carriage Hills.

Troy Highway, Street

Hwy.: The primary route to Troy, Ala. St.: The home of Troy State University; parallel to Auburn St.

Truett Drive

Honors the Baptist minister Dr. George W. Truett.

Tuckabatchee Court

Upper Creek town on the west bank of the Tallapoosa River. Derivation uncertain; ancient name is "Is-po-co-gee."

Tudor Drive

The ruling family in England (1485-1603). See "Wynton M. Blount Cultural Park."

Tulane Drive

One of the first African-American entrepreneurs in Montgomery, grocer Victor Tulane had a store at the corner of Ripley and High streets. He built the Tulane Building on the corner of High and Ripley streets and also served on the board of trustees of Tuskegee Institute. He died in 1931 and is buried in Oakwood Cemetery.

Tullibody Drive

The Scottish home of Alabama State University founder William Burns Paterson.

Tullis Drive

For Clayton Tullis, the first elected mayor of Cloverdale after it became a city in 1910.

Tunney Street

Gene Tunney defeated Jack Dempsey for the heavyweight championship in 1926 and 1917. See Dempsey St.

Turner Boulevard, Place

Blvd: One near and one on Gunter Annex of Maxwell AFB. Prev. Avenue G, redesignated in memory of 2nd Lt. Sullins Preston Turner. He left college to become a flying cadet and was assigned in 1939 to Langley Field, Va. While flying a P36 from Washington, D.C., to Langley Field, his aircraft was struck from behind by another plane in the formation and plummeted to the ground. Other blvd.: Possibly for former state senator Beloved L. Turner; when the capitol at Montgomery burned in 1849, Turner assisted in removing records from the burning structure. Pl.: Honors Julius M. Turner, an area developer.

Tuscaloosa Street

The Choctaw word that means "Black Warrior," now a river and a city in Ala., home of the University of Alabama. Some Montgomery city street names were taken at random from the Tuscaloosa map.

Tuscan Court

Tuscany is the northern region of Italy.

Tuskegee Circle

A town located E. of Montgomery, the home of Tuskegee Institute, where George Washington Carver did pioneering research on plants.

Tuttle Street

In a neighborhood of last names used for streets.

Twain Curve

According to area residents, this street was named by Dr. Tom Oliver, the former property owner. Some local business people assume that Dr. Oliver had Mark Twain in mind.

Twelve Oaks Lane

The Wilkes family plantation in Margaret Mitchell's *Gone with the Wind*. See Sturbridge.

Twin Lakes Drive (E. & W.)

Descriptive. See Twin Lakes Loop, Parkway.

Twin Lakes Loop, Parkway

The Lakewood Estates area, formerly named Twin Lakes community, was developed by Sonny Wadsworth. Three lakes are actually located in the community; the streets were given names reflecting that general motif. Eddie Barrett purchased the property and renamed the community, but not the streets.

Twining Street

Prev. 8th St. on Maxwell AFB, redesignated to honor the long, illustrious career of Gen. Nathan Farragut Twining, who served over three years as President Eisenhower's chairman of the Joint Chiefs of Staff. He was sent to Europe as an observer during WWI, but saw action in several theatres during WWII. His B-17 was shot down in the South Pacific in 1941 and Twining spent six days on a life raft before he was rescued. He retired in 1960.

Tyler Court, Road

Possibly for Col. Robert Tyler, son of U.S. President John Tyler, who was the register of the treasury for the Confederacy. He died in 1877 of paralysis at the age of 60 and is buried at Oakwood Cemetery.

U

Underwood Street

Part of W. D. Westcott's estate, Woodrow Place, in 1912. Possibly for William Thompson Underwood, a prominent Montgomery businessman in the late 1800s or Oscar Underwood, a U.S. Senator (1915-1927).

Union Circle (N., S., E., & W.) and Street (N. & S.)

Prev. Brown St. For the War of 1812 Gen. Jacob Brown, who fought at the Battle of Niagara. It was renamed Union St. sometime after 1842 for unknown reasons, but there are two theories for the change: to show contempt for the Union because the outhouses for the capitol were on this street, or an effort to appease federal government officials who occupied the area during Reconstruction.

University Court, Drive (N. & E.)

Ct.: Situated near Auburn University at Montgomery. Dr.: Located on the grounds of both Alabama State University and AUM.

Upchurch Circle

Former property owner Robert Upchurch.

Upper Wetumpka Road

One of two roads to Wetumpka. Called "upper" because of its altitude relative to the Lower Wetumpka Rd. Of the two, this road was less likely to flood.

Upton Road

In an area of English-themed names.

V

Valencia Drive

See Monterey Park.

Valerie Circle †

Valley Brook Lane

Near Whites Slough.

Van Allen Drive

The middle name of a grandson in the Vickers family, who were deeded 2,700 acres from Mt. Meigs to High St. by President John Quincy Adams.

Vance Lane

See "Montgomery's Own Philadelphia Story."

Vandenberg Street

Prev. 7th St. on Maxwell AFB, redesignated to honor Gen. Hoyt Sanford Vandenberg, the second chief of staff of the U.S. Air Force. He graduated from the U.S. Military Academy in June 1923 and earned his wings in Sept., 1924. He was flight instructor at Maxwell Field's Air Corps Tactical School, Deputy Air Commander in Chief of Allied Expeditionary Forces, and was appointed director of the Central Intelligence Agency in June 1946. Vandenberg went back to the Air Force in 1947 with four-star rank and headed the Air Force until he retired in 1953 because of illness.

Vanderbilt Loop (E. & W.)

Nashville, Tenn., university, founded in 1872. See College Grove.

Vandiver Alley, Boulevard (E. & W.), Court

Alley: For Miss Willie Vandiver, who married Louie B. Whitfield, of the Whitfield Pickle Factory family. Blvd. and Ct.: Vandiver Park was once used as a training site for the Alabama National Guard and in 1916 was designated by the federal government as a center of mobilization for WWI. This 2,000-acre tract was then purchased from Capt. A. G. Forbes to be used as a major military training site, named Camp Sheridan.

Vandy Court, Drive

A shortened version of Vandiver, a local family name, or the nickname of Vanderbilt University in Nashville, Tenn.

Vann Street

See King's Hill.

Vaughn Court, Lane, Road

For W. H. Vaughan, an Ala. legislator and landowner. "Vaughan" has often been misspelled as "Vaughn" in area street names and references.

Vaughn Lakes Boulevard

Leads to Vaughn Lakes Apts. off Vaughn Rd.

Vaughn Plaza Road

An access road to Vaughn Rd. adjacent to Vaughn Plaza Shopping Center.

Vazis Lane

George Vazis, Sr., was the film projectionist for the old Empire Theatre. His son, George, Jr., bought and developed the pecan grove now known as Country Estates in west Montgomery.

Vermont Drive

Honors the N.E. state.

Victoria Court

A Carol Villa street probably named by newer developers than the Johnson family, original landowners.

Victory Street

The area was developed during the 1940s; probably refers to WWII.

View Street

Overlooks the Alabama River.

Viking Street

See "Montgomery's Own Philadelphia Story."

Vineyard Lane

Parallel to Arbor Glen Rd. The area out Vaughn Rd. from the city was once dotted with orchards and agriculture for miles.

Vinson Road

In a neighborhood of last names used for streets.

Virgil Court

One of a group of short parallel streets bearing men's names.

Virginia Avenue

For the daughter of Philemon and Caroline Sayre, Caroline Virginia, who had two daughters, one of whom was also named Virginia.

Virginia Loop Court, Drive, Road

Amid other obvious references to the state of Va.

Vista Circle

Located on a hill and named for the view.

Vista View Drive, Place

In the Vista View community.

Volz Court

Attorney Charles Volz, an investor in Brighton Estates.

Vonora Street

The result of a contest sponsored by Jake Aronov, the real

estate developer of Capitol Heights in the 1930s. A cash prize was offered for the best entry. An unknown person won with Aronov spelled backward.

W

Wabash Street

The Wabash River that flows across north central Indiana. May be a reference to the Wabash Cannonball, since this street is near a railroad line. See also Walbash Dr., another variant of this name.

Wade Street

Named by Dora L. Bell, the property owner in the 1880s.

Wagon Park

See Arrowhead West.

Wakefield Court, Drive

In an area of names used for streets.

Wake Forest Drive

A university in Winston-Salem, N.C. that was founded in 1834. See College Grove.

Walbash Drive

A mutation of "Wabash." See Wabash St. See Bell Station.

Walker Street

An Ala. county organized in 1823 and named for Sen. John Williams Walker. Also of note: Abram Joseph Walker was chief justice of the Ala. Supreme Court (1859-65.) He died in 1872 and is buried at Oakwood Cemetery.

Wall Street

Located in a businesses area, and probably named for the N.Y. City street.

Wallace Drive (N. & S.)

Near Governors Dr. and shopping center, named for the former Gov. and presidential candidate George C. Wallace (1919-).

Walnut Street

See Maxwell AFB and Highland Park. Of note: Walnut was one of the three telephone exchanges that existed in the city prior to 1941.

Walton Drive
Son of Luther Leonidas and Laura S. Hill, former owners of the land.

Wampold Court, Road
For Charles Wampold, a local attorney and investor in Brighton Estates.

Wanda Court
A Carol Villa street that was probably named by developers after the Johnson family, original landowners. Amid other women's names used for streets.

Warbler Street
A songbird; in Westview Gardens.

Ward Street
Prev. 1st St. on Gunter Annex of Maxwell AFB, renamed to honor Cpl. Edward Ward, the first enlisted airman in the newly established Aeronautical Division Aug. 1, 1907. He was first a balloon pilot and later an aviation pilot.

Ware Court
See Wares Ferry Rd.

Ware Hill Court, Drive
See Wares Ferry Rd.

Wareingwood Drive
See Wares Ferry Rd.

Wares Ferry Rd.
One of the five ferries that once crossed the Alabama River en route to the city. Dr. Robert J. Ware, a planter and practicing physician, settled in the area once known as the Fork (above the river) around 1825. He built an imposing home and a ferry to facilitate transportation of his cotton to Montgomery; belonged to the Whig party and served in the state legislature; married a Miss White from Mobile, and they produced three offspring, Robert Y., James and Mary. He later moved to the city and "had a fine brick residence." He also owned the property that is now known as Dalraida.

Warren Court
An early Montgomery family.

Warrenton Court, Place, Road
In an area of last names used for streets.

Warwick Street

In an area of English-themed references.

Washington Avenue (E.), Street

Honors George Washington (1732-99), first president of the U.S. (1789-97). The downtown Washington Ave. continues eastward intermittently.

Washington Ferry Road

Once led to a ferry on the Alabama River that crossed to Washington, a town founded in 1817 and probably named for the first U. S. president. Washington was the Autauga County seat in 1829-30; had its own post office from 1819-35; and was virtually a ghost town by 1879. A short section of the original road is located on Maxwell AFB.

Watchman Drive

See Bell Station.

Water Street

Located on the riverfront.

Waterford Road

A possible reference to Waterford Crystal. See Regency Park.

Water Mill Road (N. & S.)

See Carriage Hills.

Water Oak Court, Lane

See Halcyon South.

Waters Edge

See Arrowhead West.

Watson Avenue, Circle, Court

Ave: For a local property owner in the 1870s. Cir., Ct.: Located in Mountainview Estates. The Watson family owned property in this area.

Watts Street

For John Watts, a landowner in 1884. Also of note: Thomas Hill Watts, governor during the Civil War years (1863-65) as well as a Confederate colonel and attorney general, was the son of John Hughes Watts, who moved to the Ala. Territory in 1818 in what is now part of Butler County. Gov. Watts was the oldest of 12 children, and in 1848 he moved his "lucrative law practice" to Montgomery, where he soon became one of the area's wealthiest cotton plantation owners. He is buried in Oakwood Cemetery. His grave marker bears these words: "Lawyer, Soldier, Statesman, Patriot. He loved his state and its people. His people loved and honored him."

Waverly Drive

For the town near Nashville, Tenn., that houses Andrew Jackson's plantation, the Hermitage. Located near Hermitage Dr.

Wayne Street

In an area of people's names used for streets.

W. D. Harris Street

A property owner in this area, and the father of City Councilman Herman Harris.

Weaver Avenue

In an area of family names used for streets.

Wedgewood Drive

The maker of English china since the 18th century. Located near other street names ending in "wood."

Well Road, Street

Rd.: Five wells that once provided the water for the city's use were located along this road. This was also the former location of J. W. Well Lumber Company. St.: Probably once the location of another well.

Wellington Road

A street amid others with historic references, this is for the "Iron Duke" (1759-1862) who defeated Napoleon at Waterloo and was later England's prime minister.

Wentworth Drive

In an area of people's names used for streets. Of note: An Australian patriot who helped to establish representative government for that country.

Wesley Drive

Probably for John and Charles Wesley, Methodist clergymen and reformers.

West Boulevard, Drive, Street

Blvd.: The western side of Montgomery's perimeter road. Dr.: Located northwest of the Inner Circle on Maxwell AFB. St.: The western boundary of the original location of the Montgomery Country Club.

Westchester Place

See Wynlakes.

Westcott Street

For W. R. Westcott, owner and developer in 1893. Also of note: David S. Westcott bought 410 acres in Montgomery at the Milledgeville land sale in 1817.

Westgate Street

Situated in the Westgate neighborhood.

Westlakes Place

See Wynlakes.

Westminster Drive

Westminster Abbey, in London, site of the monument to Shakespeare and other writers. See "Wynton M. Blount Cultural Park."

Westmoreland Street

An early planter family who first settled in the area known as "The Forks" and later moved to Montgomery. Known also as Westmoreland Ave.

Westover Road

The estate of Va. colonial official and writer William Byrd; the city of Richmond is located on the former site of one of his estates.

Westport Boulevard

A city in Conn.; located in a western area of the city.

West Ridge Court

A western street in its neighborhood.

Westview Drive

Located in the southwest part of the city.

Westwood Drive

In area of land owned by the Westcott family. Streets in the Westgate subdivision.

Wetumpka Highway

U.S. Hwy. 231 N., connecting Montgomery and the city of Wetumpka.

Weymouth Court

A bay in England painted by John Constable. See Regency Park.

Whatley Street

One of a grouping of three streets bearing surnames.

Wheeler Street
Joseph "Fighting Joe" Wheeler (1836-1906), a well-known Confederate soldier who served in Congress from 1885-1900 and as a general in the Spanish-American War of 1898.

Whetstone Drive
The maiden name of developer William Thames' wife. Located in Forest Hills.

Whipporwill Court
A misspelled version of whippoorwill, a bird that is common to the region and noted for its mournful, repeating call.

Whispering Pine Drive
In an area of pine references.

Whisper Trace Court
See Wynlakes.

Whisperwood Court, Drive
A reference to the whispering pines that are prevalent in Montgomery's neighborhoods.

Whistlewood Road
A forest reference in the Lake Forest neighborhood.

White Street
Prev. Avenue D on Maxwell AFB, redesignated to memorialize Lt. Edward O. White, the third person to be killed in an airplane accident at Maxwell. He died in June 1925.

White Acres Road
The White family owned a home and this land in Heatherton Heights. Their farm home was on Gatewood Dr.

White Bluff Court
Descriptive, generic.

Whitehall Court, Street, Parkway
A broad street between Parliament and Trafalgar Squares in London, England, along which the offices of government are located. The remains of the 17th-century palace from which the street takes its name are now used as a banqueting house.

White Oak Lane
A North American oak that is valued for its hard wood. Intersects Live Oak Ct.

White Slough Road
Perpendicular to one of the largest sloughs running through the Montgomery area, shown on maps as Whites Slough.

Whitewater Court

Usually refers to turbulent water in rapids. Located close to Stillbrook, as a contrast.

Whiting Avenue

In an area of last names used for streets.

Whitman Street

George Whitman was one of the earliest merchants in the city. He was involved in several businesses including the Wharf and Steamboat Co. and the Montgomery Hall Co. He and J. W. T. Reid were the city auctioneers during the 1830s.

Whitney Drive

The daughter of Lowder developer Jerry Wills.

Whittaker Street †

Wible Court, Run

The former location of the Wible farm, now Sturbridge Plantation.

Wickham Road †

Wilbanks Street

Honors Ben Wilbanks, a local tire distributor.

Wildbrook Circle

See Brookview Manor.

Wilderness Way

A reference to the rural character of the outlying suburbs.

Wilding Drive (W.)

A plant or animal, especially wild, transplanted to a cultivated spot.

Wildwood Drive

In the Wildwood neighborhood.

Wiley Road

Honors Wiley C. Hill, son of Luther Leonidas and Laura S. Hill, who were the former owners of the land.

Wilkinson Street

Gen. James Wilkinson captured Mobile during the War of 1812 at President James Madison's order. A Wilkinson family (possibly related) was among the earliest settlers of the area known as "The Forks."

Wilksboro Drive †

Willena Street

Honors Willena Miller, the wife of property owner C. E. Miller.

Williams Road, Street

Located in two different areas of the city where last names are used for streets.

Williamsburg Lane

A restored 18th-century Va. town that was the seat of colonial government before the American Revolution. The town is the home of the College of William and Mary, established in 1693.

Williamson Road, Street

Rd.: Located near the street of the same name. St.: Prev. 4th St. on Gunter Annex of Maxwell AFB, renamed to honor Staff Sgt. John W. Williamson, who was a member of the nationally famous "Men on the Flying Trapeze," an aero demonstration team established at Maxwell Field in 1934 by Capt. Claire Chennault. Williamson was also a member of the "Flying Tigers," a group of Americans recruited to fly for the Chinese during WWII.

Willow Street

See Maxwell AFB.

Willowbrook Court

See Sturbridge.

Willow Glen Court, Drive

Amid references to outdoor scenes.

Willow Lane Drive

See Forest Hills.

Willow Oak Lane

A little-known tree native to the South.

Willow Springs Drive

Probably named for natural features of the area.

Willowick Road

A city in Ohio on Lake Erie.

Wilmington Road †

Wilson Street

The Wilson family built a handsome antebellum home at the corner of Mildred and Pleasant streets, which was famous for its garden. Zelda Sayre Fitzgerald's bedroom overlooked this garden when she was young, and she claimed it was an inspiration to her. It is believed to be the garden described by Alabama Beggs in Zelda Fitzgerald's novel, *Save Me the Waltz*.

Wiltshire Drive

The English county where Stonehenge is located.

Wimbledon Circle, Court, Road

The internationally famous English tennis tournament, one of the grand slam titles in professional tennis. See Regency Park.

Winchester Court, Road

In Hampshire, southern England, the site of the university and the cathedral, and noted as the center of learning after the Norman Conquest.

Windemere Drive

A lake in the Lake District of England.

Winderton Drive

In an area of British-sounding names and references.

Windrush Place

A reference to the country setting from which this neighborhood was created.

Windsor Avenue

A town in England and site of some of Shakespeare's plays. This area was developed in the late 1930s about the same time that Edward VIII abdicated the throne of England for a twice-divorced American woman. His brother, George V, took the throne on Edward's scheduled coronation day and subsequently gave them the titles of Duke and Duchess of Windsor.

Windwood Drive

Among other outdoor references used for streets.

Windy Lane

In an area of first names used for streets.

Winesap Road

A variety of apple with a dark red skin. Among streets named Apple Jack and Apple Orchard. This area of the city, before development, is said to have offered miles and miles of orchards.

Winfield Court, Place

For Winston, the daughter of developer James Wilson and his wife, Wynona. See Wynlakes.

Winifred Street
Part of the D. S. Woodworth property development in the 1890s.

Winnie Street
In an area of streets bearing women's first names.

Winona Avenue
Honors Winona Watts, who married James Steptoe Pinckard, a promoter of Capitol Heights.

Winslow Lane
Of interest: Edward Winslow traveled to the New World on the *Mayflower* and was an administrator of the Plymouth Colony.

Winston Drive
An Ala. county organized in 1850 and named for Gov. John A. Winston (1833-57) of Sumter County.

Winterset Court
The title of Maxwell Anderson's 1935 play.

Winthrop Court
A part of the Winthrop family development, originally known as Winthrop's Folly. The area was so far away from town, it was considered an unwise investment at the time. Owned by E. W. Clapp in 1911.

Winton Blount Boulevard
Prev. part of Taylor Rd. When Taylor Rd was opened through to the Atlanta Hwy., the stretch in front of the post office was renamed Wynton Blount Blvd. Six months later, the name was corrected. The businesses located along this street were forced to reprint their letterhead three times within a one-year period.

Withers Street
Prev. Perry Ave. Changed to honor Susanna Claiborne Withers, the wife of Clement Comer Clay, the first chief justice of the Ala. Supreme Court, who later become governor (1835-37). See Clay St.

Witherspoon Place
John Witherspoon, who represented N.J. in the Continental Congress and in the signing of the Declaration of Independence.

Wynton M. Blount Cultural Park

In 1985, at the invitation of Winton "Red" Blount and his wife, Carolyn, the Alabama Shakespeare Festival moved to Montgomery from its original home in Anniston and became a year-round professional theatre. The new home of the Festival was built on 250 acres of land, originally part of the Blount estate, donated by the family.

The creation of this cultural park became a family project. "Red" Blount's son, Thomas A. Blount, and his associate, the late L. Perry Pittman, of Blount/Pittman and Associated Architects, designed the theater. The building is based on architectural designs of a Shakespearean contemporary, Italian architect Andrea Palladio. The family's building company constructed the theater.

The theater houses two stages: the Festival, which seats 750 theatergoers, and the Octagon, which seats 250. The professional company presents several plays in the fall and winter and then a full complement of shows in repertory from March through July.

The Alabama Shakespeare Festival, in cooperation with the University of Alabama, houses special educational and training programs through which actors and technical and managerial staff can earn graduate degrees and professional certification. The students also present productions of their own each year as well as appearing in roles in the professional shows.

Three years after the Shakespeare Festival opening, the Montgomery Museum of Fine Arts moved to a new building, also located in the Blount Cultural Park. The Museum presents a permanent collection in American art, the Blount Collection of 48 paintings—noted for its comprehensive span of American art history—and various traveling and loaned collections and exhibits.

As the area around the park built up, the developers asked the Festival administrators to provide a list of British and Shakespearean names. The developers then used the list to select names to be used for street designations.

Wolke Court
For Madonna Wolke, a local realtor.

Wood Street
In an area of last names used for streets.

Woodall Circle
Joe Woodall, a local entrepeneur, worked for Hall Bros. Dairy in the 1950s. A landowner in the city's western area had not yet named his streets and the city officials were threatening to do so. Woodall drove up in his milk delivery truck and suggested that they name a street for him. He left and thought nothing more about it until later when he drove through the area and discovered his name on the street sign.

Wood Allen Court
Possibly a combination of two last names.

Woodbridge Drive
A city in northeast N.J. settled in 1665.

Woodbrook Drive
See Brookview Manor.

Woodbury Court
Towns in Conn., Iowa, N.J., N.Y. and Tenn.

Woodcrest Drive
An entrance street to Woodcrest Estates, a neighborhood with "wood" references.

Wood Duck Drive
In an area with other duck names, such as canvasback and mallard. See Twin Lakes Loop, Pkwy.

Woodfern Drive
Ferns that thrive in the moist nutrients of the woods.

Woodforest Lane
For the terrain features and the multitude of trees in the area. See Forest Hills.

Woodglen Court
Located in Woodmere; "glen" means "valley."

Woodhaven Court
A reference to the protection of large trees.

Woodhill Court, Road
Situated near Charmwood Dr. and Green Forest Ct. and Dr.

Woodland Drive (E. & W.), Street

Among other references to woodlands existing here before the area was developed.

Woodlawn Street

A town in Md.

Woodledge Drive, Place

See Fox Hollow.

Woodley Circle, Road, Terrace

For Garrett Woodley, an early 1800s surveyor who laid out the road which runs from Pine Level to Montgomery. Emily and Eliza Woodley married into the Allen and Campbell families, respectively. See Campbell and Allendale Rds.

Woodley Park Drive

Named for the neighborhood.

Woodley Square (W.)

Adjacent to Woodley Rd.

Woodmere Boulevard, Drive, Loop

A development outside of Brooklyn, N.Y. This Montgomery neighborhood contains street names in groupings for outdoor themes and women's names, among others.

Woodpark Court, Drive

Near other tree references.

Woodrow Street

Named as part of W. D. Westcott's estate, Woodrow Place, in 1912.

Woodrun Court, Drive

Amid other "wood" names for streets.

Woodside Circle, Court, Lane

Wooded area.

Woodson Drive

One of a series of streets in the Lee High School area named by 1920s developers for women's names, natural features and family names.

Woodstock Drive

A city in Oxfordshire, site of Blenheim Palace.

Wood Vale Drive

See Fox Hollow.

Woodward Avenue

Honors Gen. Thomas Woodward, one of the first settlers in the area that would later become Montgomery and one of the dignitaries to greet Gen. Lafayette during his visit to Montgomery in 1825.

Woody Lane

In an area of "wood" references.

Worchester Court, Drive

See Georgetown.

Worley Drive

In an area of last names used for streets.

Worthing Road

The developer said he liked the name.

Wright Street

Located on Maxwell AFB, the street honors the Wright brothers, Orville and Wilbur, who first visited the city in 1910 in search of a suitable site to conduct flying experiments and to train pilots. With the help of the Commercial Club of Montgomery, Wilbur selected the farm of Frank D. Kohn on the Washington Ferry Road, which had high Indian mounds that were useful in launching the flying machines. Less than one month later, "Wright Field" was ready for use, complete with a renovated hay shed for a hangar. The city's first airfield was activated and Kohn was the first local citizen to be taken aloft.

Wynchase Circle

See Wynlakes.

Wyncrest Circle

See Wynlakes.

■ WYNDRIDGE

An east Montgomery subdivision recently developed by Lowder New Homes. The streets were named by L.N.H.'s Marketing Dept.

Wyndridge Drive

See Wyndridge.

Wynfrey Place

In an area of people's names for streets.

■ WYNLAKES

A subdivision named for developer James Wilson's wife, Wynona, and their daughter, Winston. Many of the streets were named for English cities and places. Charlie Williamson gave other streets traditional, "woodsy" names.

Wynlakes Boulevard
See Wynlakes.

Wynwood Place
See Halcyon.

X

Xenia Street
In an X-, Y- and Z-named group of streets.

Y

Yale Drive
Elihu Yale, an employee of East India Company and president and governor of Fort Saint George, Madras, gave generously to the Collegiate School in Connecticut between 1714-18. The school was chartered as Yale College in 1745. See College Grove.

Yancey Avenue
For William Lowndes Yancey (1814-1863), the "silver-tongued orator of Secession," a Confederate senator, and the Confederate minister to Great Britain. He died in 1863 at the age of 49 and is buried at Oakwood Cemetery.

Yarbrough Circle, Court, Street
Honors S. H. Yarbrough, an original owner of a large area of land known as the Pickett plat.

Yarmouth Place
A town on Cape Cod.

Yates Court
In an X-, Y- and Z-named group of streets.

Yesterhouse Drive
Named for the townhouse development featuring old-fashioned detailing.

Yoder Court
In an X-, Y- and Z-named group of streets.

Yorkshire Drive

Yorkshire is a northern county of England, once the kingdom of Northumbria.

Yougene Street, Curve

William Yougene began working for Jesse French Piano Co. while still a teenager. Later, he bought the business and in 1926 moved it near the Elite Restaurant. In 1946, he moved it again to the Gay Teague Hotel Bldg. See Capitol Heights.

Young Drive

For community leader Maggie Young-Forte.

Young Barn Road

Located on land formerly used for a large cattle enterprise, now within city limits and developed by Ida Bell Young. See Young Place.

Young Farm Court, Place, Road

See Young Place.

■ YOUNG PLACE

This subdivision is named for Ida Bell Young, of the local cattle ranching family, and has a farm, outdoor or orchard theme in its street names. Cattle ranching still takes place on adjacent land, and this was one of the last large tracts in the center of a busy residential and commercial area to be developed.

Z

Zack Court

A Carol Villa street that was probably named by newer developers than the Johnson family, original landowners.

Zelda Court, Road

The original short section of the street was named for Zelda Franco, the mother of Herman Franco, the local landowner. When Aronov extended the street and developed it, Zelda Sayre Fitzgerald was used as the inspiration for the area. See Fitzgerald Dr., Sayre St.

Zelia Stephens Court

Honors the late Dr. Zelia Stephens Evans, longtime educator and deaconess at Dexter Avenue King Memorial Baptist Church. The Zelia Stephens Early Childhood Center at Alabama State University is also a memorial to her.

Zenda Court

In an X-, Y- and Z-named group of streets.

Zephyr Hills Court, Drive

See "Montgomery's Own Philadelphia Story."

Numbered Streets

1st Street

See Boylston. Generic, numeric.

2nd Street

See Boylston. Generic, numeric. Part of series of numbered streets in Highland Park. See Highland Park.

3rd Street

See Boylston. Part of series of numbered streets in Highland Park. See Highland Park.

4th Street

See Boylston. Part of a series of numbered streets in Highland Park. See Highland Park.

5th Street

See Boylston. Part of a series of Numbered streets in Highland Park. See Highland Park.

6th Street

One of three streets in a series of numbered streets including only 6th, 8th and 9th streets. Part of a series of numbered streets in Highland Park. See Highland Park.

7th Street

See Boylston.

8th Street

One of three streets in a series of numbered streets including only 6th, 8th, and 9th streets.

9th Street

One of three streets in a series of numbred streets including only 6th, 8th and 9th streets.

14th Street

See Maxwell AFB.

84th Street

Located on Gunter Annex of Maxwell AFB, this street is named for the 84th School Squadron of the Flying Cadet Basic Training Group activated at Gunter Field in 1940 to train WWII pilots.

85th Street

For the 85th School Squadron; see 84th Street.

86th Street

For the 86th School Squadron; see 84th Street.

87th Street

For the 87th School Squadron; see 84th Street.

For more information . . .

MAPS: Go to the planning and development office in City Hall at 103 N. Perry St. A complete list of city streets is updated about once a year. It includes private streets and those in the police jurisdiction that are omitted from this book. Maps are available (for a small charge) showing current city street layouts, years in which sections of the city were annexed and the historic districts. The historic maps carry plat names, which will aid you at museums and agencies.

THE ALABAMA DEPARTMENT OF ARCHIVES AND HISTORY: Here you can do the research about famous names in Montgomery, changes in street names and neighborhood names over time and history of development. Although records are not entirely complete, there is enough information here to keep you involved in the search. The files include documents, newspaper clippings, official records, personal histories and drawings and photographs.

DEVELOPERS AND CONTRACTORS: These people are hard to find, but if you know who developed your neighborhood, a phone call may get you more information about the history of the land. Your title abstract is also a complete history of your lot's ownership and may yield nuggets of interesting information.

FRIENDS AND ASSOCIATES: The history of Montgomery's streets is tied intimately to the history of Montgomery's families, and most people who have knowledge of Montgomery's past tell their fascinating stories in terms of family relationships.

REFERENCE WORKS: A city directory tells what businesses and residences are located on city streets, along with other information; *Place Names in Alabama* recounts county, city and town histories in brief; *Indian Place Names in Alabama* describes the many Indian names which have been adopted (or twisted) by the settlers who came later and displaced the Indians from this land; the following bibliography offers other helpful sources.

Bibliography

Books, Booklets, and Pamphlets:

Alabama State Coliseum Open House and Dedication. Montgomery: 1953.

Blue, M. P. *A Brief History of Montgomery.* Montgomery: T.C. Bingham,1878.

Brown, Jerry Elijah. *Clearings in the Thicket: An Alabama Humanities Reader.* Macon: Mercer University Press, 1985.

Carmer, Carl. *Stars Fell on Alabama.* Tuscaloosa: University of Alabama Press, 1934.

City of Montgomery Annual Message and Reports. Montgomery: Brown, 1898.

Conner, Tom. *Remember When...?* Montgomery: The Montgomery Advertiser, 1989.

———. *Remember When Part II.* Montgomery: The Montgomery Advertiser, 1993.

Davidson, W.B. *A Story of the Names of the Avenues, Streets, and Parks of North Highlands.* Montgomery: Dixie, 1910.

Davis, William C. *A Government of Our Own: The Making of The Confederacy.* New York: Free Press, 1994.

Dodd, Donald B. *Alabama Now & Then.* Montgomery: The Advertiser Co., 1994.

Dodd, Donald B. W. Stewart Harris, and Patricia H. Klein. *Twentieth Century Alabama: Its History and Geography.* Montgomery: Clairmont, 1993.

DuPre, Flint O. *U.S. Air Force Biographical Dictionary.* New York: Franklin Watts, 1965.

Eaton, Clement. *A History of the Southern Confederacy.* New York: Free Press, 1954.

Ennels, Jerome A. *A Brief History of Gunter Air Force Station 1940-1980.* Montgomery: HQ Air University, Maxwell AFB, 1981.

———. *The Way We Were: A Pictorial History of Early Maxwell Air Force Base, 1918-1931.* Montgomery: HQ Air University, Maxwell AFB, 1990.

Flynt, Wayne. *Montgomery: An Illustrated History*. Woodland Hills: Windsor, 1980.

Foscue, Virginia O. *Place Names in Alabama*. Tuscaloosa: University of Alabama Press, 1989.

Greenhaw, Wayne. *Montgomery: The Biography of a City*. Montgomery: Advertiser, 1993.

Goldberg, Alfred, ed. *A History of the United States Air Force 1907-1957*. Princeton: Nostrand, 1957.

Hamilton, Virginia Van der Veer. *Alabama: A History*. New York: Norton, 1977.

Harris, W. Stuart. *Dead Towns of Alabama*. Tuscaloosa: University of Alabama Press, 1977.

Ingram, Bob. *That's The Way I Saw It*. Montgomery: B & E Press, 1986.

———. *That's The Way I Saw It II*. Montgomery: B & E Press, 1987.

Jones, James Pickett. *Yankee Blitzkrieg: Wilson's Raid Through Alabama and Georgia*. Athens: University of Georgia Press, 1976.

Jordan, Wymouth T. *Ante-Bellum Alabama: Town and Country*. Tuscaloosa: University of Alabama Press, 1987.

Junior League of Montgomery. *A Guide To The City Of Montgomery*. Montgomery: Walker, 1969.

Kennedy, Donald W., and Ronald J. Kennedy. *The South Was Right!* Gretna, LA: Pelican, 1991.

Martin, Gay. *Alabama: Off The Beaten Path*. Old Saybrook, CT: Globe Pequot, 1992.

Maurer, Maurer. *Aviation in the U.S. Army 1919-1939*. Washington: Office of Air Force History, 1987.

McMillan, Malcolm C. *The Disintegration of a Confederate State: Three Governors and Alabama's Wartime Home Front, 1861-1865*. Macon: Mercer University Press., 1986.

———, ed. *The Alabama Confederate Reader*. Tuscaloosa: University of Alabama Press, 1963.

Landmarks Foundation. *Montgomery Landmarks: A Guide to the Capitol City*. Montgomery: Wells, 1990.

Moulton, Thomas Hunter. *Moulton Family and Kinsmen: Reminiscences of the year 1857*. Montgomery: N.p. 1922.

Muskat, Beth Taylor, and Mary Ann Neeley. *The Way It Was: Photographs of Montgomery and Her Central Alabama Neighbors*. Montgomery: Landmarks Foundation, 1985.

Pickett, Albert James. *History of Alabama and Incidentally of Georgia and Mississippi*. 1851 and 1878. Birmingham: Birmingham Book and Magazine, 1962.

Pioneers of Montgomery. *Old Oakwood Cemetery: A Brief History*. Montgomery: Pioneers, 1986.

———. *One Hundred Years, One Hundred Families*. Montgomery: Pioneers, 1958.

Read, William A. *Indian Place Names in Alabama*. 1937. Rev. ed. Ed. James B. McMillan. Tuscaloosa: University of Alabama Press, 1984.

Robertson, W.G. *Recollections of the Early Settlers of Montgomery and their Families*. Montgomery: Excelsior, 1892.

Rogers, William Warren, Robert David Ward, Leah Rawls Atkins, and Wayne Flynt. *Alabama: The History of a Deep South State*. Tuscaloosa: University of Alabama Press, 1994.

Stewart, John Craig. *The Governors of Alabama*. Gretna, LA: Pelican, 1975.

Summersell, Charles Grayson. *Alabama History for Schools*. Birmingham: Colonial, 1957.

The Tintagil Club. *Official Guide to the City of Montgomery*. Montgomery: The Club, 1948.

Thornton, J. Mills, III, and Joseph Caver. *Touched by History: A Civil Rights Tour Guide to Montgomery, Alabama*. Montgomery: Black Belt Press for The Dexter Avenue King Memorial Baptist Church, the Landmarks Foundation, and the Southern Regional Council, n.d.

Williams, Ben Ames, ed. *Mary Boykin Chestnut. A Diary From Dixie. 1861-1865*. Foreward by Edmond Wilson. Cambridge: Harvard University Press, 1980.

Williams, Benjamin Buford. *A Literary History of Alabama: The Nineteenth Century*. Rutherford, NJ: Fairleigh Dickinson University Press, 1979.

Williams, Clanton Ware. *The Early History of Montgomery and Incidentally of The State of Alabama*. Ed. W. Stanley and Addie S. Hoole. Tuscaloosa: Confederate Pub., 1979.

Other sources:

Alabama Department of Archives and History Public Information Files; Microfilm Files.

County Probate Records

Maps:

County maps

Insurance maps

Municipal maps

Plat maps

Sanborn Fire maps

Montgomery City Council Minutes

Montgomery City Directories

Montgomery City Telephone Directories

Personal interviews

If You Know More . . .

Although we tried hard, we did not discover the origins of the name of every street in Montgomery. We encourage any reader with more information to share it with us for inclusion in a later edition.

Please write us with the street name and location, what you know of the street's history, the source of your information (oral history, archives document, family plat map, newspaper clipping, etc.), and your name, address, phone, and e-mail or fax number.

Write us in care of:

Who Was Dexter Avenue, Anyhow?

Black Belt Press

P.O. Box 551

Montgomery, AL 36101

Or send e-mail to:

anderson@strudel.aum.edu

blgaines@edla.aum.edu

randall_williams@black-belt.com

The Editors and Writers

Who Was Dexter Avenue, Anyhow? was researched and written as a project of a joint class in the Communication and English departments at Auburn University at Montgomery (AUM). The class was taught by **Nancy Grisham Anderson***, associate professor of English and director of composition, and* **Blair R. Gaines***, assistant professor of mass communication.*

Professor Anderson teaches undergraduate and graduate writing and editing classes. She has edited works such as *Foundation Stone* and *Family Fiction* by Lella Warren; *They Call Me Kay*, a collection of letters by Kathleen White Schad; and a college textbook, *The Writer's Audience*. In addition to a lingering interest in rabbit jokes, she enjoys leading discussion groups in public libraries, attending plays, and working in her yard.

Professor Gaines, in addition to teaching, has also worked in public relations and publications production for government and business. She was the assistant editor of the *Journal of Marketing Research* and editor for the Southern Rural Development Center. One of her previous classes produced the award-winning publication *Snapshots: Portraits of Success* for AUM.

The AUM students participating in the project included:

Ashley Gordon, a senior literature major with a minor in writing and editing, is a Montgomery native who returned to school after three years living and working in London and traveling through Europe. She also works as an assistant editor at Black Belt Press.

Nicky Kilmer completed work toward her M.Ed. degree in June 1995, ending a three-year commute from a small city in the deep recesses of south Alabama. A former newspaper editor, she is a native of Presque Isle, Maine, and now lives in Florala, Alabama, with her husband, John. She plans a career in education while continuing to indulge in her first love, writing.

Stephanie Larkins earned her B.A. in 1994 and is now enrolled in AUM's Master of Liberal Arts program. She also works at the Alabama Supreme Court and plans to attend law school. She enjoys many creative activities including intricate needle-work and writing.

Cindy Manitone graduated in 1995 and is teaching 11th grade English at Robert E. Lee High School in her native Montgomery.

Gwen S. Price is a graduate student in the alternative master's program for secondary English. She lives with her husband in Brewton, Alabama. They are expecting their first child.

Judy Beavers Sims, a returning student, is a senior English major and mass communication minor. She is also researching a historical novel with the working title *They Fell at Franklin*. A native of Bessemer, Alabama, she now lives in Montgomery with her husband, Joe.

Carole K. Whitby, a senior mass communication major, plans a career in journalism. She lives in Prattville, Alabama, with her parents and brother.